THE ALTERNATIVE AUTOIMMUNE COOKBOOK

EATING FOR ALL PHASES OF THE PALEO AUTOIMMUNE PROTOCOL

BY ANGIE ALT

WITH JENIFER BEEHLER | PHOTOGRAPHED BY TONI SNELLING

DEDICATION

I would like to dedicate this book to my grandmothers, Marcella Clark and Katie Alt. You have both instilled in me your intelligence, wit and grace, but mostly I aspire to your personal strength. The presence of my strong Montanan grandmothers has helped me grit my teeth and remain resilient in the face of more challenges than you could ever know.

Grandma Katie

Grandma Marcella

TABLE of CONTENTS

FOREWORD

BY MICKEY TRESCOTT

If you find yourself reading this book, you could be one of the 55 million Americans suffering from an autoimmune disease. You could also be suffering from unexplained symptoms and worsening health that hasn't been able to be treated by the conventional medical system. You've probably heard of the Autoimmune Protocol, an elimination diet designed to pinpoint food sensitivities and allergies for those with chronic illness. Looking at the details, though, might impart a feeling of intimidation or shock. How can I make these changes happen in my life? Is this really going to work?

In my mid-twenties, I suffered through the diagnosis of two autoimmune diseases, and the following collapse of my world as I knew it. It wasn't long before I figured out how to unravel that mess and heal my body using food and lifestyle changes as medicine. I met Angie through the blogging community when the Autoimmune Protocol was very much a fringe movement. We jumped in with both feet, before there were stories of others who had made it to the other side. Angie likes to call herself an autoimmune warrior; I like to think of us as autoimmune pioneers.

Back then there was no support for living this lifestyle. No friends you could call to complain about your visiting cousin who baked bread in your kitchen and caused a month-long regression in your progress. Nobody who would understand what it feels like to get in a fight with your husband and fall face first into a chocolate bar three weeks into your elimination diet. No, you had to do this alone, with most everyone in your life thinking you were *absolutely* crazy.

When I was first introduced to Angie's writing, I was surprised at her ability to communicate about difficult topics with honesty and soul. Because of my background as a cook, I've never had issues putting food on the table. In all honesty, food is the simpler problem—how we think about food, our bodies, and the relationships we have with others are far more complex and difficult to tackle. It was Angie who taught me how to navigate these situations with incredible ease through both her writing and our friendship.

What you will find in this book is much more than how to create allergen-free meals. Woven among a mouth-watering collection of recipes you will find topics that are not tackled in many cookbooks, starting with Angie's heartfelt storytelling about what it is like to be on an autoimmune journey. You will also learn about the mental and emotional side of healing, how to deal with anger, denial, fear, grief, and acceptance in the healing process. In addition, she also teaches us about balance, cheating, and dealing with body image issues.

It is easy to think that embarking on a dietary protocol is just about food, but when you get down to the details, food is the *easy* part—especially when you have a resource of recipes such as this one to inspire you. With this book as your guide, you will be ready to tackle not only the question of "What's for dinner," but also be prepared for the emotional journey that follows, helping you embrace recovery from all angles and setting yourself up for success.

Wishing you courage and peace as you embark on this new adventure!
Mickey Trescott, NTP

Author of The Autoimmune Paleo Cookbook
http://autoimmune-paleo.com

INTRODUCTION

Much of the information I would like to share with you is based heavily on the work of Sarah Ballantyne, Ph.D., of The Paleo Mom. Her detailed research has informed my life, my healing, and this book. Her extraordinary book, The Paleo Approach: Reverse Autoimmune Disease and Heal Your Body, is available through Amazon, as well as other retailers. You will find that the information in a few of the sections of this book, specifically, "What is AIP, Really?," "Reintroductions: A Simple How-To Guide," and the detailed charts are straightforward re-tellings of Sarah Ballantyne's life-changing approach to healing. I encourage you to learn more about her at ThePaleoMom.com.

I've been blogging since 2009, but I'm not a food blogger. I didn't spend years becoming a seasoned recipe developer and I'm not a trained chef. I'm a storyteller. I'm a solid, experienced homecook, but writing a cookbook is not something I ever thought I would do. I focus on sharing useful information wrapped in heart—stuff that others can relate to because an actual real life is behind the story. Brene Brown calls this "data with soul."

Late in 2013, I realized that a big part of the story I was telling, intentionally or not, was about food. What I ate on the Autoimmune Protocol, an elimination and reintroduction diet meant to help manage autoimmune disease, had dramatically changed my life. I had become a certified health coach and was showing other folks how to change their lives with food. I was sharing photos of my meals with a growing audience several times a week and the comment I got over and over from nervous, but willing, folks was "Your food looks real and it makes me feel like I can do this." I was inspired by the vulnerability of those comments to begin this cookbook project. People were ready to reclaim their health—they just needed to know that somebody like them, a regular person in a regular kitchen making regular food, had actually done it, too.

But I wanted to do more than write recipes. Restructuring the way I ate in an effort to heal yielded surprising results in my life and I wanted to share that story. When I first began the Autoimmune Protocol, it seemed unbearably limiting and I doubted my ability to live a full life on such a restrictive diet. I soon discovered that life is about much more than food and that healing myself actually opened, rather than closed, hundreds of possibilities for creativity, fulfillment and happiness. I wanted to write about all the other things that can happen when you change the way you eat. I wanted to share all my "data with soul."

I started to put a plan together and began talking with my friend, Mickey Trescott, author of *The Autoimmune Paleo Cookbook*. She is the sort of friend that always challenges you to press beyond your comfort zone. We have a common focus on healing through food, but we each have very unique approaches so I knew her thoughts would be valuable. She pushed me to move forward with my ideas. The spark started with the vulnerability of my readers, turned into flames thanks to a supportive friend, and within a few months, became a fire that burned me right out of my comfort zone.

I approached my younger sister, Jenifer Beehler, about collaborating with me on the project. I wanted to see if we could develop a cookbook for people with autoimmune diseases that would still appeal to folks that did not require dietary modifications. My sister does not eat a specialized diet and her insight has prevented "tunnel vision" on this project. I also felt connected to my audience over food that "looked like something they could make." I cook in a small kitchen in an average suburban home. I don't own lots of fancy equipment, my appliances are outdated and although I try to source the best quality food as often as possible, I have budgets that need to be carefully managed just like everyone else.

The final cut is over 55 delicious, inventive recipes that touch on all phases of the Autoimmune Protocol, from strict Elimination Phase dishes to recipes with ingredients from each of the four reintroduction stages (as laid out in Sarah

Ballantyne's, *The Paleo Approach*). There is food here that will please you (and your doubting in-laws) at your next family meal, plus there is room to grow as you heal and expand your dietary choices. You'll also find basics on the protocol, including helpful charts and checklists, some thoughts on many of the different facets of this journey and some very honest pieces about my own personal story.

I hope you find this cookbook to be a valuable tool in your kitchen and your heart. I want it to be helpful, inspiring, and hopefully, ease any apprehension you may have about whether or not life can still be delicious on a healing diet. Thank you for allowing me to tell these stories. I've put a lot of heart into making sure it is the *tastiest* story I've told yet.

WHAT IS AUTOIMMUNE DISEASE?

Our immune systems are miracles of nature. They swoop in like a super hero and perform incredible feats in order to save helpless on-lookers (i.e. all the cells that equal a person). Sometimes, usually for an unknown reason, this system is doing such major battle that collateral damage starts to occur and then everything goes haywire. The cells and tissues it was previously defending now look like the enemy and the immune system becomes incapable of telling the difference between good and bad. In more concise terms, autoimmune disease is the failure of the immune system to recognize the body as self. That's right. If you have an autoimmune (AI) disease, your immune system is on high alert all the time and it often mistakes you for the enemy.

AI diseases fall into two categories: organ-specific and non-organ-specific. The area the immune system was previously protecting and is now attacking defines the autoimmune disease. For instance, if your immune system suddenly stops recognizing your pancreas as

YOUR IMMUNE SYSTEM... MISTAKES *YOU* FOR THE *ENEMY*.

you and starts attacking it, you will develop type 1 diabetes, an organ-specific autoimmune disease. If the inappropriate immune response is more widespread, you might develop a non-organ specific autoimmune disease, like rheumatoid arthritis. There are 80-100 known autoimmune diseases, with 40 others suspected as autoimmune in nature as well.

The idea that the attack occurs for "an unknown reason" is more like a "sort of known reason." There is usually a genetic susceptibility and then a trigger. (It also makes a difference if you are a dude or a lady. Ladies make up 75% of those suffering from autoimmune disorders.) Triggers are not always well understood or easily identified. For instance, the American Autoimmune Related Diseases Association points out that chronic high-stress, acute high-stress events, hormones, certain drugs, viruses, bacteria and even pregnancy can act as triggers. In other cases, as with celiac disease, the trigger (gluten, a protein found in wheat, barley and rye) is well understood.

Autoimmune disease is on the rise, making awareness more important than ever. Once an autoimmune disease develops, others can follow. Approximately 25% of people with autoimmune disease develop Multiple Autoimmune Syndrome (MAS), which is defined as having three or more autoimmune disorders, usually one of which is a skin disorder. Particular autoimmunes often group together, for instance Hashimoto's thyroiditis and celiac disease. Symptoms of AI disease can be vague and are often overlooked for years allowing the disease to take hold. This makes awareness all the more critical.

The American Autoimmune Related Diseases Association says that about 55 million Americans, one in every five, have an autoimmune disorder. That's a ton of people! If you are one of them, understanding the nature of your disease is critically important on a healthcare level, but also in order to get the most out of the management approach advocated by this book. If you are not one of them, be grateful, but please, educate yourself. It is very, very likely that someone you know and care about is doing battle with autoimmune disease. Your support and understanding means a lot.

WHAT IS AIP, REALLY?

Acronyms are useful, but they suck. They make you feel like an outsider. Like everyone knows a code that you haven't been clued into yet. Even worse, in the case of AIP, which stands for Autoimmune Protocol, the acronym does not even remotely convey the true impact of this method of healing. A better acronym might be HMBTCPW, which obviously stands for "Holy Moly, Batman, This Crazy Plan Works!" Let me explain . . .

I am not a dieter. Before I got sick I had never been on a diet. Never. I'd never counted calories or points or done a 30-day challenge of any kind. In the last few months before I was diagnosed with celiac disease I had attempted a 3,000 calorie a day regimen in hopes of saving what was left of my quickly fading frame, but that was the closest I ever came to really trying to modify my food intake in any form. Deciding that I would tackle something like AIP was a huge leap for me. So what convinced me to try something so unorthodox from both a personal and societal perspective?

Honestly . . . desperation. Like many of you, my initial explorations started with a desperation-driven attempt at Paleo. It seemed crazy to remove all grain, all dairy, and all legumes from my diet, but considering that I thought I was dying, it seemed reasonable. This is not dramatic flare for the sake of storytelling. I was mentally and emotionally at the lowest point of my life. I was physically debilitated and conventional medical approaches were not working. I went to the ER on a near weekly basis with frightening, inexplicable symptoms, from numbness down the center of my face to swelling of the throat and shortness of breath. I was soon so scared and stressed from the multiple emergency room trips and baffled doctors that I could barely function. When Paleo came to my attention I thought, "it can't be worse than where I am right now."

A week after my initial attempt at Paleo, I came across Sarah Ballantyne's site, *The Paleo Mom*, and began learning about the Autoimmune Protocol. I learned that for some, basic Paleo was not enough. Those with chronic illness, particularly autoimmune disease, may benefit from a different version of Paleo —the Autoimmune Protocol—to help manage their condition. AIP works by focusing on nutrient density, gut health, hormone balancing and immune system regulation. These four areas are addressed using a strict food elimination phase followed by staged reintroductions. Five lifestyle factors are also addressed— stress management, sleep, gentle exercise, outdoor activity and support networks are prioritized for their huge impact on short and long-term well-being. Compared with the incomplete approach being taken by my doctors, all of this made perfect sense to me. I immediately recognized that this protocol was appropriate for me, but I also began to understand something else: it was *not* a diet. It was a *template*.

Diets pressure people to follow rules. Templates promote self-discovery. I began to realize that "Paleo," "Primal," "AIP," and "WAPF," were just words and acronyms describing a blueprint based on some of the food and lifestyle choices of our ancestors. Depending on my genetics, my current level of health, my resources, and my goals, I could individualize this template to heal myself. That was the moment I knew AIP would be more than an act of desperation. I no longer needed convincing. I was now on a deliberate journey of healing.

The Basics

Now that you understand the "Holy Moly, Batman" part, I can explain the basics of the template. AIP has two phases, an Elimination Phase and a Reintroduction Phase. During the Elimination Phase, AIP calls for removal of:

- Grains
- Dairy
- Legumes (including soy and peanuts)
- Eggs
- Refined/processed sugars, oils, and food additives
- Nuts and seeds (including cocoa and coffee)
- Nightshades
- Spices derived from berries or fruits
- Alcohol
- NSAIDS (nonsteroidal anti-inflammatory drugs, i.e. Advil)

Detailed charts can be found on pages 18–19 and 24–25.

It is also helpful to moderate the intake of:

- Green/black tea and yerba mate
- Salt (use mineral rich salts, i.e. pink or gray)
- Fructose (10-20 grams per day)
- Omega-6, polyunsaturated fat-rich foods (poultry and industrially raised fatty meat)
- Moderate and high glycemic load fruits/vegetables (dried fruit, plantain, taro, etc.)
- Coconut

Health can be boosted with the addition of the following healing foods:

- Bone broth
- Grass-fed organ meats
- Grass-fed gelatin or collagen
- Oily, cold water, wild-caught fish
- Fermented foods or probiotic beverages
- High quality fats

Occasionally, folks do not improve as expected once beginning the protocol. This may be due to additional food sensitivities such as high FODMAP (fermentable oligo-, di-, and monosaccharides and polyols) foods due to SIBO (small intestine bacterial overgrowth), histamine intolerance, sulfite sensitivity, salicylate sensitivity, or oxalate sensitivity. If improvements don't seem to be happening, consider learning about, and making adjustments for, these sensitivities.

After good health is firmly reestablished, a four-part process of reintroducing foods can be attempted. (Details about reintroductions can be found on page 20.) *Everyone* will need a minimum of 30 days in the Elimination Phase, many will need 3-6 months and some will need a year or more. Elimination Phase timelines are highly variable and have a lot to do with your particular condition, how severe it is at the time you begin the protocol, how long your autoimmune condition went undiagnosed (since this may have contributed to development of more AIs or damage to organs) and your personal commitment level to the process.

Just Begin

The avoid list can seem daunting, especially when first undertaking the protocol and the add list can also seem hard to stomach as most of those foods are not regular parts of a modern diet. However, if you devote ample healing time to the elimination period, add healing foods, and commit to major lifestyle improvements, results can be dramatic. AIP provides a welcome reduction in severe symptoms for many people, some even report halting or slowing the progress of their autoimmune disease. AIP can also be a powerful addition to required medications, often resulting in lower dosages and for some, the end of medication entirely.

The changes to your everyday eating can seem overwhelming, but the most urgent message I want to convey is how important it is to just get started. The same goes for the lifestyle factors. Quality in all aspects of AIP matters, but it is more important to just start. Gradually, your food choices will expand and you will figure out how to restructure your schedule in order to meet your needs for managing stress, sleeping, exercising, spending time outdoors and strengthening your support networks. Don't let perfection paralyze you and keep you from moving forward.

AIP provides a fantastic starting point for a much healthier, and yes, happier, life. If you put in the effort and patiently work to understand what your body needs, you will soon have a personalized template that promotes your bio-individual best health. You'll be thinking, "Wow! HMBTCPW!"

I know, acronyms suck, but sometimes they're just easier.

ELIMINATION PHASE
A WEEK-BY-WEEK HOW-TO GUIDE

WEEK 1	WEEK 2
grains and alcohol	*legumes and nightshades*

GRAINS

Amaranth
Buckwheat
Corn (yep, it's a grain!)
Barley (gluten, yuck!)
Kamut
Millet
Oats
Quinoa
Rice
Rye (gluten again!)
Sorghum
Spelt
Teff
Wheat (lots of gluten!)

ALCOHOL

Beer
Hard Cider
Wine
Fortified Wine
Liquor
Spirits

——————— **LEGUMES (BEANS)** ———————

Adzuki	Lentils
Black	Lima
Black-Eyed Peas	Mung
Butter	Navy
Calico	Peas
Cannellini	Peanuts (yep, legume!)
Chickpeas	Pinto
Fava	Runner
Great Northern	Snow Peas
Green	Soy (another legume!)
Italian	Split Peas
Kidney	Sugar Snap Peas

——————— **NIGHTSHADES** ———————

Ashwagandha	Pimentos
Cayenne	Sweet Peppers
Eggplant	Tobacco (yep, nightshade!)
Goji Berries	
Ground Cherries	Tamarillos
Hot Peppers	Tomatillos
Nightshade-Based Spices	Tomatoes
Pepinos	White Potatoes

NOTES

The first foods to be removed are the least nutrient-dense and the least tolerated. The last foods to be removed are the most nutrient-dense and most well-tolerated after healing. This process is basically the reverse of suggested reintroductions found in Sarah Ballantyne's, *The Paleo Approach*.

Remember that the Elimination Phase is not all about removing foods. There are foods you can still enjoy, but may need to moderate, and healing foods you should definitely add in order to maximize healing.

You may find that by week five your inflammation and pain levels have dropped to where you are able to decrease/eliminate NSAID use.

WEEK 3

dairy and coffee

DAIRY
Butter
Butter Oil
Buttermilk
Cheese
Cream
Ghee
Ice Cream
Kefir
Milk
Sour Cream
Whey
Yogurt

COFFEE
Coffee is a seed, but I find separating it from chocolate, which is also a seed, during the elimination process is easier.

WEEK 4

eggs and refined/processed sugars, oils, and food additives

EGGS
Chicken
Duck
Goose

REFINED/PROCESSED SUGARS, OILS, AND FOOD ADDITIVES
Any added sugars, including agave, high-fructose corn syrup, brown rice syrup, cane sugar, sugar alcohols, stevia, and nonnutritive sweeteners (aspartame, saccharin, etc.)

Any processed vegetable oils, including canola (rapeseed), corn, cottonseed, palm kernel, peanut, safflower, and soybean.

Any food additives, including artificial and "natural" colors and flavors, brominated oils, emulsifiers, and autolyzed and hydrolyzed proteins, MSG, nitrates and nitrites.

Basically, don't eat it if you can't pronounce it.

WEEK 5

nuts and seeds + fruit and berry-based spices

NUTS
whole, flours, butters, and oils

Almond	Macadamia
Brazil	Pecan
Cashew	Pine
Chestnut	Pistachios
Hazelnut	Walnuts

SEEDS
whole, flours, butters, and oils

Anise	Fenugreek
Annatto	Flax
Caraway	Hemp
Celery Seed	Mustard
Chia	Nutmeg
Cocoa	Poppy
Chocolate	Pumpkin
Coriander	Sesame
Cumin	Sunflower
Fennel	

FRUIT AND BERRY SPICES
Allspice
Cardamom
Juniper
Pepper (black, white, green, pink)
Vanilla Bean

REINTRODUCTIONS
A SIMPLE HOW-TO GUIDE

Reintroduction of foods after strict compliance with the Elimination Phase is often fraught with anxiety. Am I ready? How do I do this? What if I have a bad reaction? Unfortunately, this anxiety can sometimes lead to disordered approaches to eating. (More on this topic on page 84). The reintroduction process need not be cause for so much apprehension. Again, I look to Sarah Ballantyne of *The Paleo Mom* for guidance. My approach is her approach.

Am I Ready?

Being in tune with your body may be a new skill and you may still mistrust your intuition in this area. The ideal sign of readiness is full remission of your AI disease and full adoption of the lifestyle aspects of AIP. That can seem daunting, even impossible, so it helps to have more clarity on when to begin. Luckily, *The Paleo Approach* provides clear guidelines that can be useful in helping us gauge our readiness.

- You have been strictly AIP compliant for at least 30 days, three-four months is best.
- Stress, sleep, exercise, and time outdoors are all well managed.
- Your autoimmune disease is not progressing.
- You have experienced marked symptom improvement.
- You are able to digest food well without GI symptoms (even if you need digestive-support supplements).
- You can manage your autoimmune disease without DMARDs (disease-modifying antirheumatic drugs), NSAIDs (nonsteroidal anti-inflammatory drugs), or steroids. Always involve your doctor in this process (Ballantyne 329).

In what order should I try these foods?

After what might be months or even a year (or more) of determined avoidance of certain foods, it can be hard to decide in which order you will attempt reintroductions. Cravings might be strong, convenience might be a huge factor, or you may be anxious to bring in a food that has a nutrient you know is important, but was out during elimination (like eggs). With my own healing, I followed my intuition on what I suspected would work and I often give my clients the choice to work based on cravings, but there are some guidelines that are useful here, too. Please consider the suggestions below and then refer to the detailed chart on page 24.

Important things to consider:

- If you have eliminated additional foods due to conditions or sensitivities, start with those foods. This would include FODMAPS due to SIBO (small intestine bacterial overgrowth), high-histamine foods due to histamine intolerance, high-sulfite foods due to sulfite sensitivity, high-salicylate foods for salicylate sensitivity, and high-oxalate foods for oxalate sensitivity. All of these foods will generally be tolerated again if your gut is healed and they are a good place to start the reintroduction process. If you find that you still cannot tolerate them, you are unlikely to tolerate any other foods that are out during Elimination Phase. Retreat to full elimination at this time.
- If you know you have a severe allergy or a condition that prevents you from ever eating a particular food, *do not* attempt reintroduction. For instance, no amount of healing is going to make gluten okay for those with celiac disease.

See detailed Food Reaction Checklist on page 26.

How do I do this?

Let's just be real here . . . reintroducing foods is a long, tough process, however, taking the time to be methodical pays huge dividends. You will have a completely customized diet that is right for you when you finish! I tell my clients to "be an awesome scientist." Know that you are about to conduct one of the most important experiments of your life with these important steps: limit variables (strict Elimination Phase and attention to lifestyle factors), follow the procedure (outlined below), track all the data (detailed Food Reaction Checklist on page 26), and be willing to accept the conclusions, even if they disagree with the hypothesis.

Here's the procedure as per *The Paleo Approach.*
- ☐   Select a food to reintroduce.
- ☐   Start with half a teaspoon or less and wait 15 minutes. If there are reactions, stop.
- ☐   If there are no reactions, eat one full teaspoon and wait 15 more minutes. If there are reactions, stop.
- ☐   If there are no reactions, eat one-and-a-half teaspoons and wait two–three hours. If there are reactions, do not go any further.
- ☐   If there are no reactions, eat a normal portion of the food and wait three–seven days. Do not reintroduce any other foods and track reactions during this time (Ballantyne 331).

See detailed Food Reaction Checklist on page 26.

If there are no reactions, that food can be brought back into your diet and you can begin another reintroduction. Be aware that you may find a food is tolerated when you eat it occasionally, but not when eaten regularly.

| ½ tsp | 15 minutes | 1 tsp | 15 minutes | 1 ½ tsp | 2–3 hours |

What if I have a bad reaction?

This is what everyone is nervous about, right? We don't want to experience the disappointment that comes when a food reintroduction is not successful. We don't want to have such a bad reaction that the resulting flare is hard to manage. Mainly, I think we don't want to confront the fact that more healing might be necessary. I completely understand. I grappled with all of these issues during my own reintroduction process. There is a way forward, I promise you.

Firstly, reactions can vary greatly so be diligent with tracking (see detailed Food Reaction Checklist on page 26). Tracking will help you be more certain when reactions are mild and take time to build. It will also help you confidently spot a particularly bad reaction very early on and hopefully minimize any flare it may cause. Secondly, if a reaction is particularly negative, simply retreat to full elimination. Give yourself plenty of time, concentrating on healing foods, before diving back into reintroductions. While it is disappointing, it is also valuable communication from your body. Remember the days when you did not understand anything your body was saying? Now you are in full communication mode. This is good! And finally, remember that a food that did not work today may work in the future. A good example of this from my own journey are white potatoes. For a long time they did not work for me, leading to loads of joint pain in my hips. Today I can eat them a few times a week with no problems. Homemade French fries are worth the healing effort!

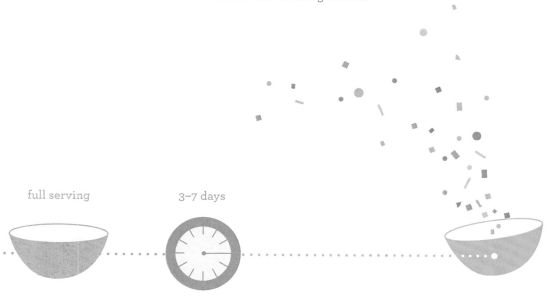

full serving   3–7 days

REINTRODUCTION PHASE
A STAGED APPROACH

STAGE 1

EGG YOLKS
Chicken

Duck

Goose

LEGUMES
beans with edible pods only

Green

Peas

Runner

Snow Peas

Sugar Snap Peas

SEED-BASED SPICES

Anise	Fennel
Annatto	Fenugreek
Caraway	Mustard
Celery Seed	Nutmeg
Coriander	Poppy
Cumin	

FRUIT AND BERRY-BASED SPICES
Allspice

Cardamom

Juniper

Pepper (black, white, green, pink)

Vanilla Bean

NUTS AND SEEDS
oils only

Macadamia

Sesame

Walnut

DAIRY
grass-fed

Ghee

NOTES

If you have eliminated FODMAPs, high-histamine foods, high-sulfite foods, high-salicylate foods, or high-oxalate foods, you will want to attempt reintroducing them before proceeding with anything outlined here.

If a food was removed during the Elimination Phase, but is not listed here, it may be that you will never want to consider reintroducing it due to its negative effects.

If you know you have a severe allergy or condition that prevents you from ever eating a particular food, do not attempt reintroduction.

The stages presented above are based on information found in Sarah Ballantyne's, *The Paleo Approach* (334).

STAGE 2

NUTS AND SEEDS
whole, flours, and butters; excluding cashews and pistachios

Almond
Brazil
Chestnut
Cocoa/Chocolate
Flax
Hazelnut
Hemp
Macadamia
Pecan
Pine
Pumpkin
Sesame
Sunflower
Walnuts

EGG WHITES
Chicken
Duck
Goose

DAIRY
grass-fed

Butter

ALCOHOL
small quantities

Gluten-Free Beer or Hard Cider-8 oz. or less
Wine-5 oz. or less
Fortified Wine-3 oz. or less
Liquor-3 oz. or less
Spirits-1 oz. or less

STAGE 3

NUTS
Cashews
Pistachios

NIGHTSHADES
Eggplant
Paprika
Sweet Peppers

COFFEE

DAIRY
grass-fed

Cream
Kefir
Yogurt

STAGE 4

DAIRY
grass-fed

Cheese
Whole Milk

NIGHTSHADES
Ashwagandha
Cayenne
Goji Berries
Ground Cherries
Hot Peppers
Nightshade-Based Spices
Pepinos
Pimentos
Tamarillos
Tomatillos
Tomatoes
White Potatoes

ALCOHOL
larger quantities

WHITE RICE

OTHER GLUTEN-FREE GRAINS
soaked and fermented

OTHER LEGUMES
soaked and fermented

FOOD REACTION CHECKLIST

SLEEP

Unable to stay awake

Unable to stay asleep

Not feeling rested
after sleep

CRAVINGS

Sugar cravings

Fat cravings

Need for caffeine

Craving minerals from
non-food items (like
chalk, dirt, or clay)

ACHES/PAINS

Muscle aches or pains

Joint aches or pains

Tendon aches or pains

Ligament aches or pains

DIGESTION

Stomach ache

Diarrhea

Constipation

Heartburn

Nausea

Gas

Bloating

Undigested food in stool

MOOD

Mood swings

Depression

Low stress tolerance

Noticeable increase in
anxiety

ENERGY

Reduced energy levels

Fatigue

Afternoon energy dips

SKIN

Rash

Acne

Pink bumps or spots

Dry hair, skin, or nails

MISCELLANEOUS

Headache (from mild to
migraine)

Dizzy or lightheaded

Phlegm, runny nose, or
postnasal drip

Coughing or constant
need to clear throat

Itchy eyes, mouth, or ears

Sneezing

Disease symptoms
returning/worsening

NOTES

Use this checklist each day for three to seven days with each new food reintroduction. If any of these reactions occur, note it in a food tracking journal like the one to the right.

The above checklist is based on similar information found in Sarah Ballantyne's, *The Paleo Approach* (330).

FOOD JOURNAL

DATE			
FOOD			
APPROX. AMOUNT			
TIME/PLACE			
PHYSICAL			
EMOTIONAL			

RECORD daily exercise & any additional thoughts here.

DENIAL IN ILLNESS & HEALING

ILLNESS AND DENIAL

I have Multiple Autoimmune Syndrome (MAS), which is defined as having three or more diagnosed autoimmune diseases. I have celiac disease, endometriosis, and lichen sclerosis. Lichen sclerosis (LS) is an autoimmune skin condition and due to its nature, most sufferers are incredibly private about their diagnosis. I am writing about it publicly for the first time here with the hope that others will feel less ashamed. Delay in diagnosis and in adopting necessary diet and lifestyle modifications increases the chances of developing further autoimmune diseases. MAS often includes a skin disorder and being open about my LS helps demonstrate that connection, which I hope will make recognition of MAS easier for others.

My autoimmune story begins with the birth of my daughter, a few months before I turned 22. Shortly after her birth, I noticed the first signs that something was wrong with me. I developed a painful condition that was changing my skin. I narrowed down what I thought it could be and armed with my knowledge, went to see my doctor. Surprisingly, he agreed. He diagnosed me with lichen sclerosis, gave me a powerful steroid cream and sent me on my way. He did not tell me that LS is an autoimmune disorder, nor did he mention that having one autoimmune disorder meant I could be susceptible to developing others.

Within a short period, I developed other problems, which I now recognize as early signs of celiac disease. I remember thinking, "What is wrong with me?" Like most AI patients, I spent much of the early part of my journey doubting myself, thinking I just needed to pull it together. It was a stroke of luck to get my LS diagnosis so easily, but nothing since then has been simple. Diagnosis is often a ridiculously long process for those with autoimmune diseases and without a name for the illness or a clear method of managing it, many patients find themselves in some form of denial. I'm no different and pushed through years of increasingly severe symptoms of celiac disease and endometriosis, refusing to hear what my body was trying to tell me.

HEALING AND DENIAL

I discovered the Autoimmune Protocol about three months after my celiac diagnosis. Fueled by desperation, I dove in headfirst. In those first weeks I thought it would be over within a few months. I believed I could follow the protocol for 30 days and reintroduce all my favorite foods soon after. To be honest, I thought AIP was my ticket back to a mostly standard American diet, minus gluten. I was in denial that restaurants, packaged convenience foods, and take-out were going to become almost non-existent for me. I threw temper-tantrums and screamed about "everything I can't eat that everyone else gets to have." I was not yet open to how much real nutrition could change my life.

MEATY MAINS

LEMON-ROSEMARY BRINED PORK CHOPS

SERVINGS 4

PREP TIME 15 MINUTES + 3 HOURS brining

COOK TIME 6 MINUTES

Ingredients

1¾ cups filtered water

5 tablespoons salt

1 yellow onion, sliced

4 garlic cloves, crushed

4 sprigs fresh rosemary

3 bay leaves

1 lemon, halved

¼ cup white wine vinegar

20 ice cubes

4 bone-in pork chops

This is currently the recipe most frequently in my weekly rotation. It is very flavorful and gets rave reviews every single time I serve it.

1. In a medium saucepan, combine water, salt, onion, garlic, rosemary, bay leaves, lemon and vinegar. Bring mixture to boil over high heat, stirring until salt dissolves. Remove from heat, cover and let sit 10 minutes.

2. Place ice in a large bowl. Pour brine over ice and stir to melt.

3. Place pork chops in a large freezer bag. Add brine and seal. To avoid spills, place bag in a large bowl and set in refrigerator for 3 hours.

4. After brining, remove chops from bag. Rinse and pat dry. Discard brine. Grill over high heat for 2–3 minutes per side. Serve and enjoy!

NOTES

Very thin-cut chops may only need 1–2 minutes per side. Pork can dry out quickly, so be careful.

BACON AND ARTICHOKE STUFFED PORK CHOPS

SERVINGS 4

PREP TIME 15 MINUTES

COOK TIME 30-40 MINUTES

Ingredients

4 thick-cut, boneless pork chops

4 slices bacon, chopped

2 cups canned (in water) artichoke hearts, quartered

salt, to taste

Crowd pleaser! This recipe is easy, but looks beautiful and makes everyone happy.

1. Preheat oven to 350 degrees. Horizontally, slice deeply into the fattiest side of each chop, creating a pocket. Set chops aside.

2. Fry bacon in a large skillet for 3 minutes over medium-high heat. Add artichoke hearts and stir. Cook until bacon is crispy.

3. Fill chop pockets with spoonfuls of artichoke and bacon stuffing. Use cut skewers or toothpicks to close pockets. With the same skillet used for the bacon and artichokes, sear each chop over medium-high heat, approximately 4 minutes per side. Place chops in a shallow baking dish. Scoop any leftover filling into dish and around chops. Bake 30-40 minutes, depending on thickness of chops. Serve and enjoy!

NOTES

Other than fresh, canned artichoke hearts packed only in water are your safest AIP option. They can be found in most grocery stores.

KALE AND PINEAPPLE BREAKFAST SKILLET

SERVINGS 4

PREP TIME 30 MINUTES

COOK TIME 20 MINUTES

Ingredients

1 pound ground pork

1 tablespoon ground ginger

6 cups rough chopped kale, stems and ribs removed

½ cup chopped green onions

¼ cup chopped red onion

1 cup pineapple chunks, fresh or packed in 100% juice only, drained

This is an awesome breakfast! I've had a few friends comment that this was one of the best breakfast dishes they'd had in a long time.

1. Using your hands, work ginger into pork. Heat a skillet over medium heat, add pork and cook thoroughly. Once cooked through, transfer pork to a clean bowl, reserving fat in skillet. Add kale to skillet, stir. Cook until tender and beginning to wilt. Transfer kale to clean bowl.

2. Using the same skillet, cook green onions 1 minute, letting them get brown and crispy. Add red onion, cook 1 minute. Turn heat to medium–high and add pineapple. Cook and stir until pineapple begins to brown slightly and juices begin to caramelize.

3. Return pork to skillet. Scrape pan to incorporate caramelized juices and cook 2 minutes. Remove from heat. Add kale, toss to combine. Serve and enjoy!

NOTES

You can easily prep all the ingredients for this skillet the night before in order to make it a quicker breakfast option.

Using only the green tops of the green onions will make this a **FODMAP FREE** dish.

HONEY-THYME BRINED PORK ROAST

SERVINGS 6

PREP TIME 5 MINUTES + 8 HOURS brining

COOK TIME APPROXIMATELY 3 HOURS

Brine Ingredients

1 (2–3 pound) pork loin roast, preferably with a good fat cap

⅓ cup apple cider vinegar

¼ cup salt

½ white onion, chopped

5 garlic cloves, crushed

2 bay leaves

3 tablespoons honey

filtered water

Rub Ingredients

3 tablespoons dried thyme (this is a lot of thyme, but trust me here!)

1 teaspoon salt

1 garlic clove, crushed

Please don't let the long brining time prevent you from making this roast. There is actually very little hands-on time and the results are incredible. This recipe is a favorite in our home, I hope it becomes one in yours.

Brine

1. Place pork in a large covered pot (slow cooker inserts work really well). In a medium bowl, whisk vinegar, salt, onion, garlic and honey. Pour over pork roast. Add bay leaves and filtered water to cover. Place pot in refrigerator 8 hours or overnight.

2. After brining, drain roast and discard brine. Rinse roast and pat dry. Set aside.

Rub

1. Preheat oven to 225 degrees. Process thyme, salt and garlic in a food processor for 30 seconds.

2. Place brined pork in a roasting pan. Coat entire roast in thyme mixture. Roast, fat cap up, until internal temperature is 145 degrees, approximately 3 hours. Allow to rest 10–20 minutes before carving. Serve and enjoy!

NOTES

It is better to underbrine than overbrine. If overnight will be longer than 8 hours for you, start the brine early in the morning instead.

PORK AND SPROUTS BREAKFAST SKILLET

SERVINGS 4-6

PREP TIME 15 MINUTES

COOK TIME 15 MINUTES

Ingredients

1 pound Brussels sprouts, thinly sliced

1 pound ground pork

1 white onion, chopped

3 garlic cloves, minced

salt, to taste

This recipe is so simple, but makes a surprisingly filling and flavorful breakfast. I often make a batch to have on hand for quick "reheat and go" meals several mornings a week.

1. Wash and trim Brussels sprouts, discarding any wilted or damaged outer leaves. Using a mandolin (or a sharp knife if you don't have a mandolin), carefully shave or slice Brussels sprouts holding them by the root end. Set aside.

2. Brown pork in a large skillet over medium heat. Once cooked through, transfer pork to a bowl, reserving fat in pan. Add onion and garlic to skillet, stir. Cook over medium heat until onion is translucent. Add Brussels sprouts, stir. Cook over medium-high heat until crisp and brown on edges. Add pork back to skillet and cook 2 minutes to reheat. Season with salt. Serve and enjoy!

DUCK FAT ROASTED CHICKEN

SERVINGS 4-6

PREP TIME 10 MINUTES

COOK TIME 1 HOUR, 20 MINUTES

*I love duck fat. Like **really** love it. I think it can give a dish richness and depth of flavor that might otherwise be lacking. Here, it takes a simple roast chicken to great new heights.*

Ingredients

1 (2-3 pound) whole fryer chicken

1 large bunch fresh herbs of choice (I prefer thyme)

salt, generous amounts

3 tablespoons duck fat, melted

1.   Preheat oven to 400 degrees. Rinse and pat chicken dry. Lay fresh herbs in the bottom of a roasting pan. Set chicken, breast side up, directly on top of herbs. Salt chicken, inside and out. Roast for approximately 1 hour and 20 minutes.

2.   Remove chicken from oven and carefully pour melted duck fat over entire chicken. Allow to rest in pan. Once cool enough for handling, carve. Serve and enjoy!

NOTES

Duck fat can be found online from retailers like *Fat Works*.

You are going to be shocked, seriously, when you try this recipe. I feed it to unsuspecting folks all the time who are then completely floored when I reveal there is no cheese or grain in the recipe. These bites make a great main dish or party snack.

"CHEESY" CHICKEN BITES WITH PESTO

SERVINGS 4

PREP TIME 45 MINUTES

COOK TIME 35 MINUTES

Pesto Ingredients

2 cups fresh basil, packed

2 garlic cloves

½ teaspoon salt

2 teaspoons fresh lemon juice

⅔ cup olive oil

Chicken Ingredients

¼ head cauliflower, "riced" in food processor (see notes)

¼ cup coconut-milk yogurt

8 slices prosciutto, sliced in half lengthwise to form long strips

1 whole chicken breast, trimmed of fat and cut into 16 bite-size pieces

1 cup tapioca flour

5 tablespoons arrowroot flour

1 cup coconut flour

5 tablespoons water

1 tablespoon thyme

3 tablespoons lard, melted (coconut oil can be substituted)

Pesto

Place all pesto ingredients in a food processor. Process until smooth. Transfer to small bowl. Set aside.

Chicken

1. Preheat oven to 350 degrees. Line a baking sheet with parchment paper. In a medium bowl, combine cauliflower "rice" and yogurt to make "cheese" mixture. Spread small amount of mixture onto 1 prosciutto strip. Place 1 chicken piece on prosciutto strip and roll into bite-size ball. Place on parchment. Repeat with all prosciutto and chicken. Set-aside.

2. Set tapioca, arrowroot and coconut flours out in three separate, shallow bowls. Mix water into arrowroot flour, stirring until arrowroot dissolves. Mix thyme into coconut flour, stir. Working with one chicken bite at a time, coat bites in tapioca flour, then arrowroot mixture, and finally coconut flour. Shake off excess flour and place bites back on parchment-lined baking sheet. Bake 30 minutes or until chicken is cooked through, turning halfway through baking. Allow to cool.

3. Melt lard over very high heat. Once chicken bites are cool, fry in hot lard for approximately 1 minute per side. Allow to drain and cool. Serve with pesto dipping sauce. Enjoy!

NOTES

• For cauliflower "rice" - chop raw cauliflower into florets. Place florets in food processor and process on high until "grainy" rice consistency is achieved. Do not pulverize.

• Coconut-milk yogurt can be found in health food stores and some grocery stores, but there are also many easy recipes online for making your own.

• Look for prosciutto brands that only include pork and salt as ingredients.

TURMERIC-TURKEY STUFFED CABBAGE ROLLS

SERVINGS 4-6

PREP TIME 30 MINUTES

COOK TIME 30 MINUTES

Ingredients

12 large green cabbage leaves

1 pound ground turkey

2 large carrots, peeled and grated

1 onion, minced

4 garlic cloves, peeled and minced

2 teaspoons turmeric

½ cup chopped, fresh cilantro

salt, to taste

This recipe has a very flavorful and satisfying filling. It is also a great dish to prepare and freeze for those days when you are too busy to prepare dinner.

1. Preheat oven to 375 degrees. Bring a large pot of water to boil. Cut core from cabbage. Submerge cabbage head in boiling water for 60 seconds. Remove from water. Leaves should be pliable and easily removed. Peel off 12 large leaves and set aside. Place remaining cabbage in refrigerator for later use.

2. In a large bowl, mix all remaining ingredients by hand. **WARNING**: *turmeric will stain.* Spoon approximately ¼ cup filling into each cabbage leaf and roll, starting at the base of the leaf and folding in sides as you go. Place each roll, seam side down, in a 9×13 baking dish. Pour ½ cup water in bottom of dish and bake 30 minutes. Allow to cool. Serve and enjoy!

ALTERNATIVE AUTOIMMUNE

BURGER STUFFED PATTY PAN SQUASH

SERVINGS 5-6

PREP TIME 20 MINUTES

COOK TIME 30 MINUTES

After receiving a truly astounding number of patty pan squash (something I'd never eaten before) in my CSA a few summers ago, I developed this recipe. I've been enjoying it each season ever since.

Ingredients

10 small-medium patty pan squash

1 pound ground beef

1 shallot, minced

1 large carrot, peeled and grated

2 garlic cloves, minced

1 teaspoon turmeric

1½ teaspoons salt

1.   Preheat oven to 350 degrees. Bring a large pot of water to boil. Using a ladle or slotted spoon, carefully lower squash into boiling water. Blanch 3 minutes. Remove from water and set aside to cool.

2.   Mix remaining ingredients by hand in a large bowl. **WARNING**: *turmeric will stain.*

3.   Cut tops off squash and scoop out insides. Discard insides and stuff squash with beef mixture. Place stuffed squash in a large baking dish and bake 30 minutes. Serve and enjoy!

BREAKFAST MEATLOAF

SERVINGS 8

PREP TIME 15 MINUTES

COOK TIME 65–75 MINUTES

Ingredients

5 slices bacon

1 small white onion, chopped

1 large carrot, peeled and chopped

3 garlic cloves, crushed

2 pounds ground beef

¼ cup maple syrup

1 tablespoon balsamic vinegar

salt, to taste

I first made this meatloaf on a trip to Montreal. It was yummy, but not quite right for dinner. During our photo shoot for this cookbook, it was suggested that it might work better as a breakfast dish. Hello and good morning! Breakfast Meatloaf was born!

Preheat oven to 350 degrees. Put bacon, onion, carrot and garlic in a food processor. Process on high 30 seconds. Transfer bacon mixture to a large bowl. Add ground beef, maple syrup, vinegar and salt. Mix all ingredients by hand and form into loaf. Place meatloaf in center of a large roasting pan. Bake 65–75 minutes. Serve and enjoy!

BACON WRAPPED ROSEMARY SCALLOPS

SERVINGS 4

PREP TIME 10 MINUTES

COOK TIME 6-10 MINUTES

Ingredients

1 tablespoon fresh rosemary leaves

2 tablespoons olive oil

1 pound scallops

1 pound bacon

salt, to taste

I created this recipe at the last minute for a Memorial Day cookout a few years ago. I was thrilled when it turned out to be a big hit. Bacon, honestly, it takes a good thing and does something cosmic to it!

1. Place rosemary and olive oil in a food processor. Process on high 30 seconds. Set aside.

2. Using a sharp knife, remove tough muscle from side of each scallop. Rinse and pat dry.

3. Wrap each scallop in 1 slice bacon. Thread wrapped scallops onto soaked wooden skewers. Grill on high heat, turning every minute until done, approximately 3 minutes for smaller bay scallops, 5 minutes for larger sea scallops. Scallops will be opaque when done. Remove from heat and drizzle with rosemary mixture while still hot. Serve and enjoy!

ANGER IN ILLNESS & HEALING

ILLNESS AND ANGER

Chronic illness is no stranger to anger. I have gone back and forth with this stage of the grieving process many times on my AI journey. Anger with my doctors and the healthcare system in general has been particularly challenging to cope with. I received so much information that was flat-out wrong that to this day, it can make my blood boil. The first misdiagnosis I received on my way to learning I had celiac disease was irritable bowel syndrome. An estimated 15% of celiacs are misdiagnosed with IBS, leading to a damaging delay in proper treatment. As you can imagine, when I first considered all the needless pain I had been through, I was furious thinking of how I had been dismissed early on with the "it's just IBS" label.

I faced similar problems trying to get a name for endometriosis. It was not until three years after my husband and I first started trying to have a baby that I learned about it, despite seeking help at one of the nation's leading fertility clinics where we provided an extensive health background, including family medical history, all of which pointed to endometriosis. All manner of tests were run, but it was not suggested I be evaluated for endometriosis. When all of our results came back normal we were urged toward expensive, invasive fertility treatments. We questioned the doctor, our primary concern now moving beyond fertility. "Could there be something more serious wrong with me?" we asked. The doctor told us that my age, 29, was a factor in our declining fertility. I found this information utterly depressing, especially as many friends, all in the same age range, began having babies with apparent ease while I suffered through excruciatingly painful periods every month. Later, I learned that a huge number of women who experience secondary infertility have endometriosis. In fact, it is one of the top three causes of infertility in general. Learning that sent me into a rage for months. I felt my husband and I had been cheated out of the family we so dearly wanted.

HEALING AND ANGER

Once I embraced AIP, I began healing very quickly. Incredibly, I experienced complete relief from my crippling anxiety and panic attacks within 72 hours of being on the protocol. The power of the gut-brain connection was abundantly clear to me at that point. Most of my worst symptoms healed in the following months and my gluten antibody numbers dropped rapidly, reaching the normal range six months after I started the protocol. By the time I hit the one year mark, I was in a completely different place, but even with all those positive developments, still there was anger. I was angry at all the misinformation I had been given about food. I was angry that I was going to have to live in a world filled to overflowing with temptation, and I was angry that doing the right thing for my body was so much work. But anger is a part of healing, and I *was* healing, that much was clear.

STAGE 1

MAPLE-MUSTARD PORK ROAST

SERVINGS **6**

PREP TIME **15 MINUTES**

COOK TIME **APPROXIMATELY 3 HOURS**

! REQUIRED REINTRO
• MUSTARD, BLACK PEPPER

Ingredients

1 (2–3 pound) pork loin roast, preferably with a good fat cap

6 tablespoons mustard

4 garlic cloves, minced

1 tablespoon dried thyme

1–2 tablespoons maple syrup

1 teaspoon salt

½ teaspoon black pepper

This roast is such a big hit in the home of one of my friends that her kids call it, "Miss Angie's Pork." That's me, spreading the love of pork wherever I can!

1. Preheat oven to 225 degrees. Rinse roast and pat dry.

2. In a small dish, combine all remaining ingredients. Coat entire roast in mustard mixture.

3. Roast, fat cap up, until internal temperature reaches 145 degrees, approximately 3 hours. Allow to rest 10–20 minutes before carving. Serve and enjoy!

NOTES

Most prepared mustards list paprika as an ingredient or the mysterious "spices," which normally means paprika. Look carefully for brands that use only mustard or turmeric and mustard.

TARRAGON PORK BURGERS

SERVINGS 4

PREP TIME 10 MINUTES

COOK TIME 16 MINUTES

! REQUIRED REINTRO
• BLACK PEPPER

Ingredients

1 pound ground pork

1 tablespoon dried tarragon

1 teaspoon salt

½ teaspoon black pepper

Tarragon is a wonderful herb to add to pork. The scent and flavor are both delicious.

In a large bowl, mix all ingredients by hand. Form 4 large patties. Grill on medium heat, approximately 8 minutes per side. Serve and enjoy!

NOTES

This recipe can easily be made Elimination Phase compliant by omitting the black pepper.

STAGE 1

CHICKEN AND BOK CHOY STIR-FRY

SERVINGS 2-3

PREP TIME 35 MINUTES

COOK TIME 25 MINUTES

! REQUIRED REINTRO
BLACK PEPPER

Ingredients

3 tablespoons coconut oil, divided

1 head bok choy, washed and chopped

3 garlic cloves, minced

1 (1 inch) piece fresh ginger, peeled and minced

1 large skinless, boneless chicken breast, cubed

1 white onion, chopped

3 carrots, peeled and chopped

1 yellow squash, halved lengthwise and chopped into half moons

1 tablespoon fish sauce

1 tablespoon coconut aminos

1 tablespoon water

1 tablespoon arrowroot flour

salt and pepper, to taste

I love stir-fry, but it can be tricky to serve when rice and other grains are not on the menu. Cauliflower rice is a wonderful option, but truthfully, it's kind of messy and lots of work. When I am not feeling up to the cauliflower rice challenge, this is how I serve stir-fry. In fact, this is how I serve it most of the time—it's that good!

1. Melt 1 tablespoon of coconut oil in a warm skillet. Add bok choy, cook and stir over medium heat for 2 minutes. Add garlic and ginger. Stir, scraping pan, until bok choy is fragrant and wilted, approximately 3-4 minutes. Transfer bok choy to a bowl, cover and set aside.

2. Using the same skillet (there's no need to wash it), melt 1 tablespoon coconut oil. Add cubed chicken and cook (scraping pan) until tender and no longer pink, approximately 5–7 minutes. Transfer cooked chicken to a clean bowl and set aside.

3. Using the same skillet once again, add final tablespoon of coconut oil and melt over high heat. Add onion and cook, stirring constantly, for 3 minutes. Add carrots, cook and stir 3 minutes. Add squash and cook 3 minutes. Turn heat to medium-low. Add cooked chicken. Stir.

4. In a small dish, mix fish sauce, coconut aminos, water and arrowroot flour, stirring until arrowroot dissolves. Pour sauce over chicken & vegetables, stirring quickly until mixture begins to thicken. Remove from heat.

5. Divide bok choy into 2 or 3 servings. Spoon chicken and vegetables over plates of bok choy. Salt and pepper to taste. Enjoy!

NOTES

This recipe can easily be made Elimination Phase compliant by omitting the black pepper. For fish sauce, I prefer gluten-free *Red Boat* brand, which can be purchased online. Coconut aminos and arrowroot flour can be found in health food stores.

ZUCCHINI-CILANTRO TURKEY BURGERS

SERVINGS 4

PREP TIME 15 MINUTES

COOK TIME 16 MINUTES

! REQUIRED REINTRO
BLACK PEPPER

Ingredients

2 medium zucchini

1 pound ground turkey

½ cup fresh cilantro, chopped

2 garlic cloves, minced

salt and black pepper, to taste

Our recipe tester does not like zucchini, but she ended up loving these burgers so much that she served them again at a big family get-together. I'd say that's a big win!

1. Grate zucchini with the grating blade of a food processor or a standard cheese grater. Pile grated zucchini onto a clean cotton dishtowel. Roll towel and twist both ends tightly until water begins to drain out of zucchini. Remove as much moisture as possible.

2. In a large bowl, mix all ingredients by hand. Form 4 large patties. Grill on medium heat, approximately 8 minutes per side. Serve and enjoy!

NOTES

This recipe can easily be made Elimination Phase compliant by omitting the black pepper.

BACON-BURGER MEGA MEATBALLS

SERVINGS 4

PREP TIME 20 MINUTES

COOK TIME 30 MINUTES

! REQUIRED REINTRO
BLACK PEPPER

Ingredients

3–4 slices bacon

½ large white onion, chopped (optional)

½ cup crimini mushrooms, chopped (optional)

1 pound ground beef

salt and pepper, to taste

Our recipe tester was so happy with this dish, and so surprised at how eagerly all four of her normally picky eaters gobbled it up, that she actually called me to gush. We love these meatballs, too and often have them for breakfast. Yep, breakfast!

1. Preheat oven to 350 degrees. Fry bacon to desired crispness. Transfer to a paper towel-lined plate. Set aside to drain and cool. Reserve grease in skillet.

2. If using onion and mushroom, cook in the skillet with reserved bacon grease. Transfer to a paper towel-lined dish. Set aside to drain and cool.

3. Once bacon is cool enough to handle, rough chop and transfer to a large bowl. Add ground beef, onions and mushrooms (if using), salt and pepper. Mix all ingredients by hand in a large bowl. Form into 12 large meatballs. Place each meatball into the cup of a muffin tin and bake 30 minutes. Serve and enjoy!

NOTES

This recipe can easily be made Elimination Phase compliant by omitting the black pepper.

Removing onion and crimini mushrooms will make this a **FODMAP FREE** dish.

HOMEY BEEF STEW

SERVINGS 4-6

PREP TIME 45 MINUTES

COOK TIME 7-8 HOURS

! REQUIRED REINTRO
PEAS, BLACK PEPPER

Ingredients

1 pound beef stew meat, cubed

salt and black pepper, to taste

1 tablespoon tallow (coconut oil can be substituted)

2 medium onions, chopped

6 garlic cloves, minced

2 turnips, peeled and chopped into ½ inch pieces

4 carrots, peeled and chopped into ½ inch pieces

2 tablespoons carrot and beet puree (peel, chop and boil 1 carrot and ½ beet until soft, process in food processor until smooth)

4 tablespoons tapioca flour

2 tablespoons white wine vinegar

2 tablespoons balsamic vinegar

4 tablespoons water

2 teaspoons fresh thyme, minced

4 cups beef bone broth

2 bay leaves

1 cup frozen peas

¼ cup fresh parsley, chopped

Almost every slow cooker beef stew recipe I come across calls for tomato and potato. Nightshades are often difficult for folks to reintroduce so I was motivated to create an AIP version. I think you'll find this as comforting as I do.

1. Heat tallow in a large skillet over medium-high heat. Season beef with salt and pepper. Add to skillet and cook approximately 6 minutes. Remove from heat and transfer beef to slow cooker. Add onions, garlic, turnips and carrots, stir to combine.

2. In a small dish, whisk together tapioca flour, vinegars and water. Stir until tapioca dissolves. Heat carrot/beet puree in skillet over medium heat, add tapioca mixture. Whisk until thickened. Add thyme and beef broth, whisking until mixture is smooth, about 3-4 minutes. Pour mixture into slow cooker, add bay leaves, cover and cook on low 7-8 hours.

3. In last 30 minutes of cooking, remove bay leaves and add frozen peas. Stir. Season with parsley. Serve and enjoy!

NOTES
This recipe can easily be made Elimination Phase compliant by omitting the peas and black pepper.

LAMB KABOBS WITH ARTICHOKE HEARTS AND KALAMATA OLIVES

SERVINGS 4-6

PREP TIME 20 MINUTES

COOK TIME 20 MINUTES

! REQUIRED REINTRO
WHITE PEPPER

I have the pleasure of living right next to a big, beautiful farm where they raise organic, grass-fed lamb. My farmer is awesome and for me, it just doesn't get any better than knowing exactly where my food is coming from. I think you'll find that this preparation for ground lamb is super tasty.

Ingredients

1 pound ground lamb

1 tablespoon dried oregano

zest of 1 lemon

juice of ½ lemon

1 teaspoon salt

½ teaspoon white pepper

6 artichoke hearts, halved

24 kalamata olives, pitted

1. Mix first six ingredients by hand in a large bowl. Form into 12 large meatballs. Assemble kabobs, alternating meatballs, artichokes and olives on soaked wooden skewers.

2. Set grill to medium heat. Brush grate with oil to prevent sticking. Cook kabobs, 10 minutes per side. Serve and enjoy!

NOTES

This recipe can easily be made Elimination Phase compliant by omitting the white pepper.

Other than fresh, canned artichoke hearts packed only in water are your safest AIP option. They can be found in most grocery stores.

ORANGE SHRIMP STIR-FRY

SERVINGS 4

PREP TIME 25 MINUTES

COOK TIME 10 MINUTES

! REQUIRED REINTRO
• GREEN BEANS, BLACK PEPPER

This is an outstanding stir-fry. I would choose it over take-out any day of the week, but I understand if you miss eating out of little boxes. They are fun! To remedy the situation, just purchase some of those boxes and serve this stir-fry in them. Voila! Homemade take-out!

Stir-Fry Ingredients

1 pound shrimp, peeled and deveined, tails removed

zest and juice of 1 large orange

2½ tablespoons minced garlic

1 tablespoon minced fresh ginger

2 tablespoons coconut oil, divided

1 yellow summer squash, cut into ¼ inch slices

1 cup chopped broccoli

1 cup trimmed green beans

½ cup diced onion

½ cup peeled and chopped carrot

salt and black pepper, to taste

Sauce Ingredients

1/3 cup bone broth (beef or chicken)

1 tablespoon coconut aminos

1 tablespoon fish sauce

Stir-Fry

1. In a wok or large skillet, melt 1 tablespoon coconut oil over medium-high heat. Add shrimp and cook until opaque, about 2–3 minutes. Transfer shrimp to a large bowl.

2. Using the same wok or skillet, melt remaining tablespoon coconut oil. Add squash, broccoli, onion, carrot, orange zest and juice. Stir and cook until vegetables are tender, about 5 minutes. Add vegetable mixture to shrimp.

Sauce

Deglaze the pan with broth, scraping up any browned bits. Simmer broth 1-2 minutes, allowing liquid to reduce. Add aminos and fish sauce, simmer 1 minute. Add shrimp and vegetable mixture back to pan, stir to coat. Serve and enjoy!

NOTES

This recipe can easily be made Elimination Phase compliant by omitting the green beans and black pepper. The photo shows the dish with green beans omitted.

For fish sauce, I prefer gluten-free *Red Boat* brand, which can be purchased online. Coconut aminos can be found in health food stores.

STAGE 1 | FODMAP FREE

GRILLED SHRIMP AND PINEAPPLE SLAW

SERVINGS 4-6

PREP TIME 15 MINUTES

COOK TIME 5 MINUTES

! REQUIRED REINTRO
BLACK PEPPER

Slaw Ingredients

½ head purple cabbage, shredded

2 large carrots, peeled and grated

1 pineapple, peeled, cored and diced

2-3 tablespoons fresh cilantro, chopped

2 tablespoons apple cider vinegar

2 tablespoons olive oil

2 tablespoons grated fresh ginger

juice of 1 lime

Shrimp Ingredients

1 pound shrimp, peeled and deveined, tails removed

salt and black pepper, to taste

My sister, Jenifer, really took this recipe and made it special. It is so easy, but has tons of flavor and looks gorgeous on the plate.

Slaw
In a large bowl combine cabbage, carrots, pineapple and cilantro. In a small dish, combine vinegar, oil, ginger and lime juice. Pour dressing over cabbage mixture. Toss to combine. Set aside.

Shrimp
Thread shrimp onto soaked wooden skewers. Season with salt and black pepper. Grill on medium-high heat, approximately 2–3 minutes per side. Serve warm shrimp atop cabbage slaw. Enjoy!

NOTES

This recipe can easily be made Elimination Phase compliant by omitting the black pepper.

FISH TACOS WITH MANDARIN ORANGE AND AVOCADO SALSA

SERVINGS 4

PREP TIME 10 MINUTES

COOK TIME 8 MINUTES

! REQUIRED REINTRO
• BLACK PEPPER

Like stir-fry, tacos can be a tough go if grains are not a dietary option. This recipe came out of my desire, no, my need, to share yummy tacos with my family while also keeping everything safe and AIP legal. It was a challenge, but I'm happy to tell you that it worked and everyone loved it! I hope you do, too!

Salsa Ingredients

1 (15 ounce) can mandarin oranges, packed only in water or juice

1 ripe avocado, diced

2 tablespoons chopped fresh cilantro

½ tablespoon olive oil

½ tablespoon lime juice

⅛ teaspoon salt

⅛ teaspoon black pepper

Fish Ingredients

4 (6 ounce) white fish fillets, such as cod

2 tablespoons coconut oil

¼ teaspoon black pepper

¼ teaspoon salt

1 garlic clove, grated

1 tablespoon minced onion

Salsa
Gently combine all salsa ingredients in a medium bowl. Set aside.

Fish
1. Heat coconut oil in a large skillet over medium heat. Season fish with remaining ingredients. Cook in skillet until opaque throughout, approximately 3–4 minutes per side. Transfer to a plate and flake fish for tacos.

2. Serve with "tortillas" and salsa. Enjoy!

"Tortilla" Options
There are many Paleo recipes for tortillas available online. They are a good option, but most include egg so be aware that you will need that reintroduction under your belt before attempting these versions. Other options for "tortillas" are coconut or plantain wraps, large lettuce leaves or cabbage leaves. Pictured here is a Paleo tortilla from a recipe I found online. It worked for me, but the recipe did include egg. I encourage you to experiment with the available recipes and find one that makes you happy. After all, tacos are happy food!

NOTES
This recipe can easily be made Elimination Phase compliant by omitting the black pepper.

ROSEMARY ELK TENDERLOIN WITH HUCKLEBERRY SAUCE

SERVINGS 4

PREP TIME 15 MINUTES

COOK TIME 35 MINUTES

! REQUIRED REINTRO
• BUTTER

Looking for something very unique, that looks and tastes gourmet, but is shockingly easy to prepare? Look no further. Elk and huckleberries were staples of my life in Montana. This preparation takes these favorites to the next level.

Elk Ingredients

1 pound elk tenderloin (beef or bison can be substituted)

2 teaspoons chopped fresh rosemary, plus 2 sprigs

salt and black pepper, to taste

2 tablespoons lard (coconut oil can be substituted)

Sauce Ingredients

1 shallot, minced

1 teaspoon minced fresh thyme

½ cup fruity red wine (Pinot Noir works best)

⅔ cup beef bone broth

¼ cup + 2 tablespoons fresh or frozen huckleberries (blackberries can be substituted)

1 tablespoon butter, cold

Elk

1. Heat a cast–iron skillet over high heat for 2 minutes. Meanwhile pat elk dry and season with chopped rosemary, salt and pepper. Add lard to skillet, melt. Add elk and rosemary sprigs to skillet. Sear 4 minutes per side, until well browned and crusted.

2. Transfer elk and rosemary sprigs to a clean plate. Loosely tent with foil.

Sauce

1. Lower heat under skillet to medium. Add shallots and thyme, cook until soft, about 2 minutes. Increase heat to high and add wine to deglaze pan, scraping up any browned bits. Reduce wine by half, about 3 minutes. Stir in broth and huckleberries. Crush berries into sauce with wooden spoon. Reduce heat and simmer until sauce coats back of spoon.

2. Remove from heat and stir in cold butter. Spoon sauce over elk to serve. Enjoy!

NOTES

This recipe can easily be made Elimination Phase compliant by substituting coconut oil for butter and omitting the black pepper. Yes, it is "legal" to cook with alcohol while following Elimination Phase guidelines.

MUSTARD CHICKEN WINGS

SERVINGS 4

PREP TIME 15 MINUTES

COOK TIME 30 MINUTES

! REQUIRED REINTRO
• BUTTER AND MUSTARD

Ingredients

2 pounds chicken wings and drummets

½ cup butter, melted

2 garlic cloves, crushed

1 teaspoon dried thyme

1 tablespoon apple cider vinegar

4 tablespoons mustard

I came to a point in my AIP journey where I realized that I really wanted to eat wings with my family again, but the nightshades that seemed inherent to the dish weren't possible. I was doing well with mustard though so I started playing around, trying to find a combination of flavors that would work. This recipe is my reward. Wing night is back!

1. Preheat oven to 450 degrees. Place chicken in a large pot, cover with water and boil 8 minutes. Drain chicken and set aside.

2. In a food processor, process all remaining ingredients on high for 30 seconds. Pour ¼ of sauce into a separate bowl and set aside. Pour remaining sauce over chicken and toss to coat.

3. Place wings on a wire rack set in a large baking sheet. Bake 30 minutes. Remove from oven and coat with remaining sauce. Serve and enjoy!

NOTES

Most prepared mustards list paprika as an ingredient or the mysterious "spices," which normally means paprika. Look carefully for brands that use only mustard or turmeric and mustard.

COFFEE AND BALSAMIC RUBBED ROAST BEEF

SERVINGS 6-8

PREP TIME 10 MINUTES

COOK TIME APPROXIMATELY 2 HOURS

! REQUIRED REINTRO
• COFFEE

Ingredients

1 (4 pound) beef rump roast

½ teaspoon salt

½ teaspoon fresh ground black pepper

1 tablespoon tallow, melted (coconut oil can be substituted)

⅓ cup white onion, minced

4 garlic cloves, minced

1 teaspoon dried thyme

1 tablespoon ground coffee

1 tablespoon balsamic vinegar

Coffee and balsamic vinegar may sound like an odd combination, but honestly, it works and as an added bonus, it smells absolutely divine while it's cooking. This roast will have the whole family running to the kitchen to find out what's for dinner.

1. Preheat oven to 450 degrees. Rinse beef and pat dry. Set in center of a large roasting pan.

2. Using a food processor, process all remaining ingredients on high for 30 seconds. Coat entire roast with coffee mixture. Return roast to center of pan and set in oven. Immediately reduce temperature to 250 degrees.

3. Roast until internal temperature of meat is 150 degrees, approximately 2 hours. Allow to rest 10–20 minutes before carving. Serve and enjoy!

FEAR IN ILLNESS & HEALING

ILLNESS AND FEAR

There is one word I would use to describe the three years prior to my celiac diagnosis . . . fear. By the time I reached 30, my autoimmune journey was significantly picking up speed. My symptom severity was noticeably worsening with new symptoms developing every few months. Doctors seemed to be useless and I had far more questions than answers. Intellectually, I knew I should be in the prime of my life, but physically it felt like my body was giving out on me.

Considering the long list of symptoms, it is easy to understand my fear. Emotional instability, crying, angry outbursts and anxiety that I couldn't control, hair loss, weight loss, and mind-numbing fatigue all plagued me. Mild depression set in and with it the sense that I was "missing my self." Then truly scary things started to happen—muscle spasms in my back and legs, terrible bone pain, especially in my rib cage, and swollen glands. Sometimes I had a hard time speaking. I couldn't get words out or I stuttered. I couldn't concentrate. My senses of smell and taste seemed to be failing and my eyes were watery and blurred. My fine motor skills were diminishing, too. I would find myself unable, after six or seven attempts, to pick up a pen I had dropped on the floor.

Then came the numbness in my legs (which later spread to my arms, hands, and the center of my face), heart palpitations, painful digestive problems and dizziness. I would wake up drenched in sweat every night, panic-stricken. I did not understand that many of these things were the effects of malnourishment from celiac disease. Without a name for my problems and after seeing doctor after doctor trying (and failing) to get help, I began seeing a psychologist and a psychiatrist. One afternoon I burst into tears in the psychologist's office and mustered the confidence to ask, "Am I having a nervous breakdown?" I was terrified. We began discussing plans for me to admit myself to a psychiatric facility for a short stay.

HEALING AND FEAR

Discovering AIP was a godsend. The relief that came with healing—true healing—began to slowly drain away the fear that had been drowning me. I knew almost immediately that it was worth it, all of it, but there was a nagging new fear itching to be addressed. "Will it always be like this?" was a phrase often on my mind. It was the food restrictions, of course. I was scared that my food choices would be limited forever. Over time and with a careful reintroduction process, I was able to broaden my dietary horizons, but at the outset I was terrified that my life would forever be ground beef and broccoli.

There were other new fears, too. In the beginning, it was social events. There are almost no social gatherings that don't involve food. The big holidays? Forget about it. Every one of them is entirely (or almost entirely) centered on foods I couldn't eat during the Elimination Phase. It felt so limiting. I was afraid of being left out or worse, viewed as a nutcase. I don't practice Future Food Focused Event Fear anymore, but I remember the awful panic. The hard truth is, the road to recovery requires mustering a little, or a lot, of courage.

A SHORT WORD ABOUT BALANCE

So what exactly do I mean by balance? Well, I don't think anyone should be any more food restricted than is absolutely necessary. It is easy to lose perspective and spiral into uncompromising, even harmful, food relationships when adopting restricted eating protocols. It starts innocently. We want to heal. We really, really want to feel better. Food restriction protocols (such as AIP) help so we think, "Okay, I'll do it one better." If restricting these foods worked, then I'll restrict more foods and I'll add other kinds of healing diets because more is better. This is where balance becomes very important. More is not always better, especially if it refers to more restriction. Unnecessary levels of restriction can head in the direction of disordered eating in a hurry.

It is my belief, based both on my experience as a patient and my work as a health coach, that healing must always be holistic. Holistic healing means paying attention to the whole person, including the social and mental facets of his or her life. Considering all aspects of a person forces balance, balance that is particularly important if healing includes the use of elimination and reintroduction protocols like AIP.

The Autoimmune Protocol is an elimination and reintroduction approach to food meant to help manage autoimmune disease. A strict Elimination Phase allows our immune systems to calm and ideally aids healing, relief from symptoms and maybe, hopefully, even remission. Depending on the severity of the disease, length of illness, and breadth of damage, your Elimination Phase may be long or short. The key words here are *phase* and *reintroduction*. We are not meant to live the remainder of our lives severely food restricted.

If you've embarked on a healing journey using AIP or another food restriction protocol, it can be helpful to check in with yourself from time to time to assess things holistically. If the social or mental parts of your life seem a bit off balance, that might be an indicator that your dietary protocol is verging on disordered. If you notice yourself edging toward unhealthy territory, please seek help. There are many trained professionals that can help you address these harmful patterns. You can start by contacting the National Eating Disorders Association.

I absolutely believe in the healing power of food. I know AIP and many similar protocols work wonders for many forms of illness and are in no way "disordered eating," but walking the line between food as medicine versus food as fear can be tricky. My hope is that we can all approach healing with diet and lifestyle with a spirit of enjoyment and transformation. After all, this journey is about restoring our best selves, not developing burdened hearts and minds.

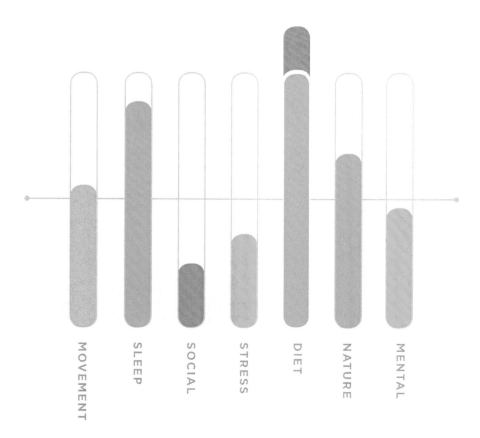

MOVEMENT   SLEEP   SOCIAL   STRESS   DIET   NATURE   MENTAL

SOUPS AND SIDES

TOM KHA GAI

SERVINGS 6

PREP TIME 1 HOUR
(including cooking chicken)

COOK TIME 20 MINUTES

Ingredients

1 (2-3 pound) fryer chicken, whole

3 quarts filtered water

1 white onion, chopped

2 bay leaves

1 teaspoon dried thyme

2 stalks fresh lemongrass, chopped

1 (1 inch) piece fresh ginger, peeled and chopped

zest and juice of 1 lime

1 cup shiitake mushrooms, chopped

1 can full fat coconut milk

2 tablespoons fish sauce

1 teaspoon honey

2 cups spinach

1 bunch fresh cilantro, to garnish

Many Thai recipes are easily adapted to a Paleo template, but it can be a little trickier with AIP. Given how much I love Thai food, creating a safe and delicious Thai recipe was a challenge I was happy to tackle. This soup turns out beautifully and comes in super handy when the Thai food craving hits. By the way, gai is pronounced, "guy."

1.   Clean and rinse chicken. Place in a large stockpot and cover with 3 quarts filtered water. Turn heat to medium–high and bring to boil. Add onion, bay leaves and dried thyme. Cook, uncovered, until chicken is tender, about 30–40 minutes. In last 10 minutes of cooking, add lemongrass, ginger, lime zest and juice.

2.   Remove chicken from pot and set aside to cool. Strain stock into a second large pot. Discard solids (lemongrass, ginger, etc.). When chicken is cool, removed meat from bones and rough chop. Bones and cartilage can be reserved for bone broth.

3.   Bring stock back to boil, add chicken meat and mushrooms. Reduce heat and simmer 20 minutes.

4.   Add coconut milk, fish sauce, honey and spinach. Simmer 3 minutes. Garnish with cilantro. Serve and enjoy!

NOTES

For fish sauce, I prefer gluten-free *Red Boat* brand, which can be purchased online.

CINNAMON MEATBALL AND SWEET POTATO SOUP

SERVINGS 6-8

PREP TIME 40 MINUTES

COOK TIME 15 MINUTES

Ingredients

1 pound ground beef

1 tablespoon ground cinnamon

3 carrots, peeled and grated

2 teaspoons salt, divided

2 tablespoons minced white onion

3 large sweet potatoes, peeled and chopped

1 cup full fat coconut milk

5 cups beef bone broth

I have a very dear friend in West Africa, Nancy, who introduced me to the delights of beef with cinnamon. I would never, ever have thought this combination could be so tasty without her to lead the culinary way. She inspired this dish.

1. Preheat oven to 350 degrees. Using your hands, combine beef, cinnamon, grated carrot, 1 teaspoon salt and onion in a large bowl. Roll mixture into bite-size meatballs. Place in a baking dish and bake, uncovered, 25 minutes.

2. While meatballs are baking, place sweet potatoes in a large pot and cover with water. Boil until fork tender. Drain. Place cooked potatoes, coconut milk, broth and 1 teaspoon salt into a food processor. Process on high until smooth. Return sweet potato puree to pot.

3. Add cooked meatballs to sweet potato puree, stir. Cook over medium heat until warmed, approximately 15 minutes. Serve and enjoy!

CANADIAN BRUSSELS SPROUTS

SERVINGS 4-6

PREP TIME 15 MINUTES

COOK TIME 40-50 MINUTES

Ingredients

1 pound Brussels sprouts

2 tablespoons coconut oil, melted

4 slices bacon, chopped

2 tablespoons maple syrup

salt, to taste

There's maple syrup in this recipe. So Canadian. Hehe! Get it? Canadian friends, please forgive my dorky sense of humor.

1. Preheat oven to 375 degrees. Wash and trim Brussels sprouts, discarding any wilted or damaged outer leaves. Chop in half.

2. Place all ingredients in a large bowl. Stir to coat.

3. Spread sprouts in a single layer on a parchment-lined baking sheet. Bake 40–50 minutes or until golden brown and crispy on edges. Serve and enjoy!

ELIMINATION PHASE

PESTO SHRIMP CUCUMBER ROLLS

SERVINGS 20

PREP TIME 30 MINUTES

Ingredients

2 large cucumbers

2 cups fresh basil, packed

2 garlic cloves

½ teaspoon salt

2 teaspoons fresh lemon juice

⅔ cup olive oil

1 pound cooked shrimp, coarsely chopped

½ cup diced celery

½ cup diced white onion

These rolls are so yummy and so very easy. They make an awesome light appetizer before a big meal.

1. Use a mandolin to carefully slice cucumbers lengthwise. Set aside.

2. Combine basil, garlic, salt, lemon juice and olive oil in a food processor. Process until smooth. Add shrimp, celery, and onion. Process on high 30 seconds.

3. Lightly spread filling onto cucumber strips and roll. Secure roll with toothpick or skewer. Serve and enjoy!

NOTES

A mandolin is really the best tool for this recipe. If you do not have one, a potato peeler or cheese slicer, held very steady, will be your best bet.

CREAMY GINGER-LIME CEVICHE

SERVINGS 4

PREP TIME 20 MINUTES

**REFRIGERATION TIME
30 MINUTES**

Ingredients

1 pound shrimp, peeled and deveined, tails removed

2 tablespoons salt

juice of 1 lime

juice of 1 lemon

1 cup finely chopped red onion

2 tablespoons grated fresh ginger

½ cup full fat coconut milk

1 cup chopped fresh cilantro

1 cucumber, peeled and diced

1 ripe avocado, diced

I had two versions of ceviche for this book and then my brilliant sister said, "Combine them." Thank goodness for sisters, because this combined version became a big hit with everyone.

1. In a large pot, boil 4 quarts of water with 2 tablespoons salt. Add shrimp and cook 1–2 minutes *maximum*. (Over-cooking shrimp will make them rubbery.) Drain shrimp and place in a bowl of ice water to halt cooking.

2. Drain shrimp and cut each in half. Place shrimp in a glass or ceramic bowl (not metal). Add lemon and lime juice. Cover and refrigerate 30 minutes.

3. Remove from refrigerator and add onion, ginger and coconut milk. Stir gently.

4. Immediately before serving, add cilantro, cucumber and avocado. Toss gently. Serve and enjoy!

HONEY AND ROSEMARY GLAZED CARROTS

SERVINGS 4

PREP TIME 15 MINUTES

COOK TIME 15 MINUTES

Ingredients

½ pound large carrots, peeled and halved lengthwise

¼ cup water

¼ cup honey

½ tablespoon chopped fresh rosemary

Very easy, but very elegant. This dish looks so lovely at a sit-down holiday meal.

Place carrots in a large skillet with water. Cover and simmer 10 minutes over medium-low heat. Uncover. Add honey and rosemary. Simmer 5 minutes. Serve and enjoy!

TURMERIC AND GINGER ROASTED CAULI STEAKS

SERVINGS 4

PREP TIME 15 MINUTES

COOK TIME 25-30 MINUTES

Ingredients

2 tablespoons lard, melted (coconut oil can be substituted)

1 teaspoon ground ginger

1½ teaspoons turmeric

1 head cauliflower

Salt, to taste

Simple and yummy! Here's a totally different way to prepare cauliflower.

1. Preheat oven to 425 degrees. Combine lard, ginger and turmeric in a small bowl. Remove leaves of cauliflower, keep core intact. Place cauliflower, core side down, on a non-slip cutting surface. Use a large, sharp knife to slice 1 inch thick "steaks."

2. Lay cauliflower slices on a parchment-lined baking sheet and drizzle each side with turmeric mixture. Season with salt. Roast until edges are crispy and browned, 25–30 minutes. Serve and enjoy!

ELIMINATION PHASE

SHALLOT AND ROSEMARY ROASTED BUTTERNUT SQUASH

SERVINGS 4-6

PREP TIME 15 MINUTES

COOK TIME 30 MINUTES

Ingredients

1 butternut squash, peeled, seeded and diced

2 shallots, diced

3 tablespoons coconut oil

1 teaspoon dried rosemary

1 teaspoon salt

Butternut squash is naturally very sweet. I had tried every sweet preparation out there and one afternoon while I was wrestling with cutting one up, (Why does cutting a butternut squash require the strength of a body builder?) I realized I was sick of sweet. I had a shallot and some rosemary on hand and this recipe came of it. I wonder how many recipes are inspired by being sick of something. I'm guessing a lot!

1. Preheat oven to 400 degrees. Put diced squash in a large bowl and drizzle with oil. Add shallots, rosemary and salt. Stir to coat.

2. Spread squash in a single layer on a baking sheet. Roast 30 minutes, stirring halfway through for even browning. Serve and enjoy!

TWICE FRIED PLANTAINS WITH ARUGULA GUACAMOLE

SERVINGS 4

PREP TIME 15 MINUTES

COOK TIME 20 MINUTES

Plantain Ingredients

2 large semi-ripe plantains (not green, but not black)

½ white onion, chopped

coconut oil or lard, for frying

salt, to taste

Guacamole Ingredients

1 large ripe avocado

1 cup chopped arugula

½ cup chopped fresh parsley

2 garlic cloves, crushed

juice of 1 lime

2 teaspoons apple cider vinegar

I was not a plantain fan prior to adopting AIP. Now I love them, especially dipped in peppery Arugula Guacamole.

Plantains

1. With peel on, cut plantains into 2 inch sections. Slice vertically into peel on 1 side of each section. Pull peel up and around section. (This is the easiest way to peel plantains.)

2. In a large skillet, heat oil to frying temperature over medium–high heat. Using a slotted spoon, gently place plantains in oil. Fry until just browned on each side. Transfer to a plate to cool.

3. Once plantains are cool, use the back of a spatula to gently press down on each section until it flattens into a patty. Return patties to hot oil. Add onion. Fry plantains until each side is deep golden brown and onions are translucent and crispy at edges. Transfer all to a plate. Cool and drain. Season with salt.

Guacamole

Put all ingredients in a food processor and blend until smooth. Transfer to a small dish. Serve with twice fried plantains and enjoy!

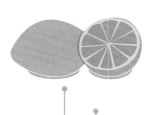

LEMONY ROASTED BRUSSELS SPROUTS

SERVINGS 4-6

PREP TIME 10 MINUTES

COOK TIME 30-40 MINUTES

Ingredients

2 pounds Brussels sprouts, halved

4 tablespoons lard or coconut oil, melted

zest and juice of 1 lemon

3 garlic cloves, minced

salt, to taste

The sharp tang of lemon goes perfectly with the light bitterness of a roasted Brussels sprout. This dish is a favorite of both my husband and daughter and is in heavy rotation at our house.

1. Preheat oven to 400 degrees. Wash and trim Brussels sprouts, discarding any wilted or damaged outer leaves. Put sprouts in a large bowl and drizzle with fat. Add lemon juice and zest, garlic and salt. Stir to coat.

2. Spread sprouts in a single layer on a baking sheet. Roast 30–40 minutes, stirring every 15 minutes for even browning. Serve and enjoy!

SAUTÉED RAINBOW CHARD

SERVINGS 4

PREP TIME 10 MINUTES

COOK TIME 7-8 MINUTES

Ingredients

2 large bunches rainbow chard (approximately 2 pounds), tough stems removed, leaves cut into long ribbons

1 (1 inch) piece fresh ginger, peeled and minced

1 tablespoon coconut oil

salt, to taste

It does not get easier than this recipe. In no time at all you'll have a delicious and very nutritious veggie to serve with any main course.

Melt coconut oil in a skillet over medium heat. Add chard and ginger, stir. Cook until chard is wilted and liquid evaporates, about 7–8 minutes. Season with salt. Serve and enjoy!

GRIEF IN ILLNESS & HEALING

ILLNESS AND GRIEF

Shortly after my 30th birthday, my husband and I reached one of our major life goals. We moved our little family to Africa. Unfortunately the timing coincided with the most extreme years of my chronic illness. Living in two of the least economically developed countries on the planet, Guinea and Sierra Leone, while deeply rewarding, was also incredibly frightening with my mounting health problems. Health scares combined with extremely limited access to medical care resulted in three terrifying medical evacuations and ultimately lead to one of the most heart-wrenching decisions of my life. Only three years after we had achieved it, I had to admit to my adventurous partner and myself that I was too ill to continue our dream. The fallout of that decision had an enormous impact on our marriage and my self-worth.

When I returned to the United States, I earnestly began seeing one doctor after another trying to get answers. I was finally referred to a GI specialist who did a gluten antibody blood screen, followed by an endoscopy, to examine my small intestine. On the morning of the endoscopy, after I woke up from the procedure, the doctor came to speak to us. With four words and in less than 10 seconds, she ended my torment. "You have celiac disease." I was 33 years old.

I started to cry . . . with relief. I was not losing my mind. I was not making this up. Something really was wrong. Very wrong. It had taken 11 years, hospital stays on three continents, more than 25 doctors and countless pokes, prods and exams, but I finally had a diagnosis. My relief was short-lived as tears of grief soon followed my tears of relief. I was grieving all that I had lost to my autoimmune diseases and what it meant for my future.

HEALING AND GRIEF

As the months passed, I became more and more comfortable following AIP. My health was steadily improving and I was no longer in denial about how much real food was changing my life. My anger had receded and I had overcome my fear about this new way of eating. What I didn't know was that mourning was as big a part of healing as it was illness. The grief over foods I had lost would hit me suddenly and leave me fighting sadness for days.

Eating is an unavoidable fact of existence. We eat in order to survive, but we also eat for the joy of it. Food and eating are knitted into important moments in our lives and memories. I soon realized that learning a new way of eating was about much more than simple will power, it meant exploring a whole complex set of emotions and memories. During my grieving process, I started sorting food and memory in my brain. In one "folder" I would put the actual food, in the other, I put the memory or significance that went with the food. Soon I found my food-based grief fading and I didn't have to develop "yummy amnesia" in order to do it. Although eating certain foods did not contribute to my good health, I didn't have to lose the memory associated with everything from my Montana heritage, holiday celebrations, or the surge of excitement that came with adulthood. The memories and emotions were in me, not the foods that accompanied them.

KALE AND LEEK SOUP

SERVINGS 6-8

PREP TIME 1 HOUR

COOK TIME 20 MINUTES

! REQUIRED REINTRO
WHITE PEPPER

Ingredients

1 pound ground pork

2 leeks, chopped (white and light green parts only)

3 garlic cloves, minced

1 large zucchini, sliced into half moons

3 cups rough chopped kale, stems and ribs removed

1 teaspoon white pepper

2 teaspoons oregano

1 teaspoon salt

zest of 1 lemon

4 tablespoons white wine

4 tablespoons water

1 can full fat coconut milk

3 cups chicken bone broth

This soup is a great way to eat lots of veggies in one sitting. I often eat it for breakfast. The warm, creamy texture is a great way to start the day.

1. In a large skillet over medium heat, cook pork, breaking meat apart for even browning. Cook thoroughly, then set aside, reserving fat in skillet.

2. Add leek, garlic and zucchini to skillet with reserved fat, stir. Cook until vegetables begin to brown. Add kale, stir. Cook until kale begins to wilt. Add pepper, oregano, salt, lemon and wine, stir. Simmer until liquid cooks down, approximately 5 minutes.

3. Transfer pork and kale mixture to a large pot. Add water, coconut milk and broth. Bring to boil, then reduce heat and simmer 5 minutes. Serve and enjoy!

NOTES

This recipe can easily be made Elimination Phase compliant by omitting the white pepper. Yes, it is "legal" to cook with alcohol while following Elimination Phase.

STAGE 1 | FODMAP FREE

TURMERIC PUMPKIN SOUP WITH SHRIMP

SERVINGS 4

PREP TIME 20 MINUTES

COOK TIME 20 MINUTES

! REQUIRED REINTRO
• BLACK PEPPER

Ingredients

1 pound shrimp, peeled and deveined, tails removed

2 cups pumpkin puree

2 cups full fat coconut milk

1⅓ cups chicken bone broth

1 teaspoon turmeric

½ teaspoon ground ginger

½ teaspoon maple syrup

1 teaspoon sea salt

½ teaspoon black pepper

This soup is not only beautiful to look at, but also beautiful to taste. Even better, my teenage daughter loves it and requests it often.

1. Bring a large pot of water to boil. Add shrimp and cook 1–2 minutes *maximum*. (Over-cooking shrimp makes them rubbery.) Drain shrimp and place in a bowl of ice water to halt cooking.

2. In a clean, large pot, add all remaining ingredients, stir well to combine. Cook over medium heat 10–15 minutes. Drain iced shrimp and add to soup. Stir to reheat. Serve and enjoy!

NOTES

This recipe can easily be made Elimination Phase compliant by omitting the black pepper.

BACON AND BRUSSELS SPROUT SEAFOOD SOUP

SERVINGS 6-8

PREP TIME 30 MINUTES

COOK TIME 25 MINUTES

! REQUIRED REINTRO
BLACK PEPPER

Ingredients

1 pound Brussels sprouts, thinly sliced

5-6 slices bacon

1 white onion, chopped

2 garlic cloves, minced

zest and juice of 1 lemon

4 cups chicken bone broth

1 pound frozen mixed seafood

1 cup white wine

2 teaspoons salt

1 teaspoon black pepper

1 teaspoon dried thyme

This was one of my earliest recipe creations after starting AIP, but it is one that I keep coming back to. If you like breakfast soups, you might find it hits the spot.

1. Wash and trim Brussels sprouts, discarding any wilted or damaged outer leaves. Using a mandolin (or a sharp knife if you don't have a mandolin), carefully slice Brussels sprouts into approximately ⅛ inch slices.

2. Fry bacon to desired crispness in a large skillet over medium-high heat. Transfer to a paper towel-lined plate, reserving grease in pan. Add Brussels sprouts, onion, garlic, lemon zest and juice to skillet, stir. Cook, continuing to stir, until sprouts are browned and onion is translucent.

3. Pour chicken broth into a large pot and bring to boil. Rough chop bacon and add to broth. Add Brussels sprouts mixture and frozen seafood. Return to boil. Add wine and remaining seasonings. Stir well. Reduce heat and simmer 15 minutes. Serve and enjoy!

NOTES

This recipe can easily be made Elimination Phase compliant by omitting the black pepper. Yes, it is "legal" to cook with alcohol while following Elimination Phase.

SPICED SWEET POTATOES

SERVINGS 4

PREP TIME 15 MINUTES

COOK TIME 55 MINUTES

! REQUIRED REINTRO
ALLSPICE

Ingredients

2 pounds sweet potatoes, peeled and cut into ½ inch pieces

1 tablespoon coconut oil, melted

¼ cup blackstrap molasses

¼ cup fresh squeezed orange juice

½ teaspoon ground cinnamon

¼ teaspoon ground ginger

¼ teaspoon ground allspice

¼ teaspoon salt

1 teaspoon pure vanilla extract

Do you want your home to smell like heaven and please some hungry mouths at the same time? This recipe will do both every time.

1. Preheat oven to 375 degrees. Place cut potatoes in a large bowl. In a small dish, combine all other ingredients, whisk well. Pour dressing over potatoes and toss to coat.

2. Place potatoes in a large baking dish, cover. Bake 40 minutes. Remove from oven and stir. Bake 15 minutes longer, uncovered. Serve and enjoy!

NOTES

This recipe can easily be made Elimination Phase compliant by omitting the allspice. The flavor is still amazing.

TART RADISH AND FENNEL SALAD

SERVINGS 4

PREP TIME 15 MINUTES

COOK TIME 15 MINUTES

! REQUIRED REINTRO
BLACK PEPPER

Dressing Ingredients

2 tablespoons lime juice

2 tablespoons honey

Salad Ingredients

1 fennel bulb, thinly sliced

1 cup sliced radishes

1 cup green apple, thinly sliced

salt and black pepper, to taste

I don't really like fennel, but surprisingly, I really like this salad. The flavor is so fresh and tangy.

Dressing
In a small dish, mix lime and honey until honey dissolves. Set aside.

Salad
Wash and trim fennel bulb and radishes. Wash and core apple, cut in half. Using a mandolin (or a sharp knife if you don't have a mandolin), carefully slice fennel, radishes and apples into approximately ⅛ inch slices. Place vegetables and fruit in a large bowl. Toss gently with dressing. Allow to sit 15 minutes as the dressing will slightly pickle the salad. Serve and enjoy!

NOTES

This recipe can easily be made Elimination Phase compliant by omitting the black pepper.

SAUTÉED PURPLE CABBAGE

SERVINGS 6

PREP TIME 8 MINUTES

COOK TIME 8 MINUTES

! REQUIRED REINTRO
BLACK PEPPER

Ingredients

1 head purple cabbage, sliced

½ large white onion, sliced

4 garlic cloves, minced

1 tablespoon lard (coconut oil can be substituted)

salt and black pepper, to taste

I have a confession . . . prior to AIP, I had no idea that cabbage could be eaten any way other than coleslaw. Sad, I know. Sautéed cabbage is as simple as it gets and so delicious! I'm so glad I know now!

Melt lard in a large skillet over medium heat. Add sliced cabbage and onion to skillet. Cook until just crisp and tender, approximately 5 minutes. Add garlic, salt and pepper, stir. Cook 3 minutes. Serve and enjoy!

CUCUMBER SPAGHETTI SALAD

SERVINGS 4-6

PREP TIME 10 MINUTES

COOK TIME 30-40 MINUTES

! REQUIRED REINTRO
• BLACK AND WHITE PEPPER

Ingredients

1 spaghetti squash, halved and seeded

¾ cup pitted kalamata olives, halved

2 cucumbers, peeled and sliced

1 small red onion, diced

1 cup small broccoli florets

1 tablespoon capers

2 garlic cloves, minced (more if you love garlic)

1 tablespoon lemon zest

¼ cup lemon juice

¼ cup olive oil (add more if salad is too dry)

white and black pepper, to taste

I don't know about you, but in my pre-celiac days I loved pasta salad. This recipe is just as yummy and offers up loads of healthy veggies in every serving.

1. Preheat oven to 350 degrees. Place squash halves into large baking dish with the cut side facing down. Bake 30-40 minutes. Remove from oven and set aside to cool. Once cooled, scrape spaghetti squash into a large bowl with a fork.

2. Add olives, cucumbers, onion, broccoli, capers and garlic to squash. Toss to combine.

3. In a small bowl, combine lemon zest and juice. Whisk in olive oil and season with pepper. Drizzle dressing over squash mixture and toss to coat. Refrigerate to meld flavors or serve immediately. Enjoy!

NOTES

This recipe can easily be made Elimination Phase compliant by omitting the black and white pepper.

STAGE 1

PEPPERY DUCK FAT SWEET POTATO WEDGES

SERVINGS 4

PREP TIME 5 MINUTES

COOK TIME 40 MINUTES

! REQUIRED REINTRO
BLACK PEPPER

Ingredients

3-4 large sweet potatoes, scrubbed and cut into wedges

½ cup duck fat, melted

½ tablespoon each, salt and pepper

Have I mentioned that I love duck fat? Delish! This recipe is a not-so-boring way to prepare sweet potatoes, which I know are an AIP staple and can get a little bland.

1. Preheat oven to 450 degrees. Place potato wedges in a large bowl, drizzle with fat, salt and pepper. Stir to coat.

2. Arrange potatoes in a single layer on two parchment-lined baking sheets. Bake in top third of oven until browned, crisp, and cooked through, approximately 40 minutes. Turn potatoes halfway through cooking to ensure even browning.

NOTES

This recipe can easily be made Elimination Phase compliant by omitting the black pepper.

Duck fat can be found online from retailers like *Fat Works*.

STAGE 2

RASPBERRY-ALMOND SHAVED SALAD

SERVINGS 6-8

PREP TIME 25 MINUTES

! REQUIRED REINTRO
ALMONDS

This crunchy salad is a great dish to bring when you are invited to eat somewhere. It looks very formal, but is easy to throw together.

Ingredients

½ cup sliced almonds, toasted

1 pound Brussels sprouts, thinly sliced

½ head cauliflower, thinly sliced

2 tablespoons fresh mint, sliced into thin strips

1 cup raspberries

3 tablespoons olive oil

3 tablespoons lemon juice

salt, to taste

1. Preheat oven to 350 degrees. Spread sliced almonds in a single layer on an ungreased baking sheet. Bake 5-7 minutes or until browned.

2. While almonds are toasting, wash and trim Brussels sprouts, discarding any wilted or damaged outer leaves. Wash and core cauliflower. Chop cauliflower into several large florets. Using a mandolin (or a sharp knife if you don't have a mandolin), carefully slice Brussels sprouts and cauliflower florets into approximately ⅛ inch slices.

3. Combine sliced sprouts, cauliflower, mint, almonds and raspberries in a large bowl. Add olive oil and lemon juice, toss to coat. Season with salt. Serve and enjoy!

NOTES

This recipe can easily be made Elimination Phase compliant by omitting the almonds. The photo shows the salad with almonds omitted.

STAGE 2 | FODMAP FREE

MASHED GINGER PARSNIPS

SERVINGS 4-6

PREP TIME 5 MINUTES

COOK TIME 15 MINUTES

! REQUIRED REINTRO
BUTTER

Ingredients

2 pounds parsnips, peeled and chopped

1 tablespoon peeled and grated fresh ginger

2 tablespoons butter

¼ cup beef bone broth

salt, to taste

My family adores parsnips and would never have discovered them without AIP. Also, and they don't know this, but this recipe is one of the ways I sneak bone broth (which they don't love) into their diets. Shhhh!

Boil parsnips in a large pot until soft, approximately 12–15 minutes. Drain. Put parsnips, ginger, butter, and broth into a food processor. Process on high 1 minute. Sample. If mash is too thick, add more bone broth, 1 tablespoon at a time, and process until desired consistency is reached. Add salt to taste. Serve and enjoy!

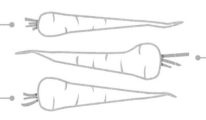

STAGE 4

FLAVOR BOMB CHICKEN AND RICE SOUP

SERVINGS 6-8

PREP TIME 2 HOURS

COOK TIME 30 MINUTES

! REQUIRED REINTRO
• WHITE RICE

Ingredients

1 (2-3 pound) whole fryer chicken

3 quarts filtered water

1 white onion, chopped

juice of 1 lemon

2 bay leaves

1 teaspoon dried thyme

1 cup peeled, chopped carrots

1 cup chopped celery

1 cup chopped green onions

4 garlic cloves, minced

1 tablespoon grated fresh ginger

1 tablespoon coconut oil

1 tablespoon fresh thyme, minced

1 tablespoon parsley

2 teaspoons salt

2 cups cooked white rice

Adding grains back into your diet may be tricky, but for some, the addition of starchy white rice after an ample healing period can be a welcome reintroduction. This recipe is great way to add it for an occasional starch source.

1. Place chicken in a large stockpot, cover with 3 quarts filtered water. Turn heat to medium–high and bring to boil. Add onion, lemon juice, bay leaves and dried thyme to pot. Cook at a slow boil, uncovered, until chicken is tender, about 30–40 minutes.

2. Remove chicken from pot and set aside to cool. Strain stock into a second large pot. Discard solids. When chicken is cool, remove meat from bones and rough chop. Bones and cartilage can be reserved for bone broth.

3. Bring stock back to a boil. Meanwhile, melt coconut oil in a skillet over medium–high heat. Add carrots, celery, green onions, garlic and ginger, stir. Boil 5 minutes. Add carrot mixture, chicken meat, fresh thyme, parsley and salt. Reduce heat and simmer 20 minutes. Remove from heat. Stir in rice. Serve and enjoy!

NOTES

This recipe can easily be made Elimination Phase compliant by omitting the white rice.

MY BUTT MANIFESTO

Have you noticed something? You only have one butt. It is extremely likely that you will only ever have just the one. What a butt should be, and look like, is something our world has numerous opinions on (although, no butts have ever requested those opinions be shared) and chances are, your butt does not measure up. Your butt may be:

too fat	too short
too thin	too jiggly
too big	too stiff
too small	too lumpy
too round	too firm
too flat	too soft
too long	too boney

My butt, by the current standards of perfection, (which, by the way, change constantly) is woefully inadequate. However, after noticing that I had just the one, I decided to judge my butt by new standards. I was delighted to learn that my butt measures up beautifully. My butt:

- provides a comfortable surface on which to sit.
- serves its primary function of elimination for my digestive system.
- provides stability to my pelvic region when moving.
- gives my hips the capacity to operate normally.
- allows me to jump and move my legs forward.
- identifies me as part of the human species through its familiar form.

Wow! High-five butt!

It may be that you, like me, have judged several other parts of your body by unrealistic standards that have nothing to do with the actual function that body part serves. Perhaps, like me, you have also accused malfunctioning body parts of deliberate sabotage. Now is the time to step back and think. Our wounded bodies are doing the best they can. Those parts are the only parts we will ever have. What would you do if you were told that you must have a spotless kitchen while your house was on fire? That's crazy, right?

It's all so unjust! Gosh! It's surprising our bodies don't band together in revolt and demand more reasonable treatment. Perhaps, before that happens, we can start to love our bodies. Perhaps we can agree to judge our bodies by appropriate standards, recognizing them for the miracle they are each living minute. Perhaps we can show mercy to parts that are broken and seek to heal them with nourishing foods and kind treatment.

That, folks, is my butt manifesto and it applies to my whole body. It is the only body I will ever have, my one and only home for my entire life so I'm going to love it, every last inch.

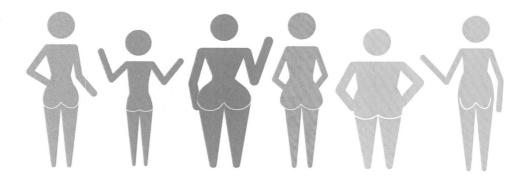

DRINKS AND DESSERTS

ALTERNATIVE AUTOIMMUNE

SUNRISE SMOOTHIE

SERVINGS 2

PREP TIME 5 MINUTES

Ingredients

1 large peach, pitted and sliced

5 cherries, pitted

1 tablespoon powdered collagen

½ cup strong black tea

1 cup full fat coconut milk

4 ice cubes

I did not realize until two years into my AIP journey that the protocol is coffee-free, but not caffeine-free. Wow! Huge realization! Admittedly, limiting caffeine is still smart, but enjoying something with a little "get up and go" from time to time is nice.

Place all ingredients in a blender. Blend until smooth. Serve and enjoy!

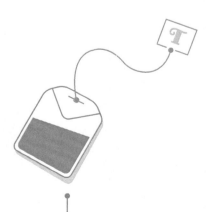

NOTES

For collagen, I prefer a high-quality brand like *Great Lakes*. It dissolves in hot or cold liquid, but does not gel like gelatin. It gives this smoothie some balancing protein. *Great Lakes* collagen can be found online.

ALTERNATIVE AUTOIMMUNE

ORANGE BLOSSOM AND HONEY PARFAIT

SERVINGS 4

PREP TIME 10 MINUTES

**REFRIGERATION TIME
AT LEAST 3 HOURS**

Gelatin Ingredients

2 teaspoons unflavored gelatin

1 cup water, divided

¼ cup honey

juice of 1 orange

Whipped Cream Ingredients

1 (15 ounce) can full fat coconut milk

½ teaspoon honey

There aren't a ton of AIP Elimination Phase desserts, so even the lightest, simplest ones are a pleasure. This recipe has the added benefit of healing gelatin.

Gelatin

1. Pour ¼ cup of water into a small bowl, sprinkle gelatin over to soften. Set aside.

2. In a small pot, bring remaining ¾ cup water, honey and orange juice to boil. Add gelatin and stir to dissolve. Pour gelatin mixture evenly into 4 pretty serving dishes or glasses. Refrigerate to set, at least 3 hours.

Coconut Whipped Cream

1. Do not make whipped cream until immediately before serving gelatin. Chill can of coconut milk in refrigerator overnight to cause water and cream to separate. Chill a glass bowl and the beaters of an electric mixer in freezer for 30 minutes before whipping.

2. When gelatin is set and ready to serve, carefully remove coconut milk from refrigerator. Do not slosh can or cream will remix with water. Open can carefully and scoop cream only into chilled bowl. Beat cream on high until peaks form, about 2–3 minutes. Add honey with beaters running. Spoon or pipe whipped cream quickly onto gelatin for layered effect.

NOTES

I prefer high-quality gelatin, like *Great Lakes* brand, which can be found online.

This coconut whipped cream recipe is based on the best method I have found, which was created by Danielle Walker of *Against All Grain*.

ROSEMARY TEA TIME BISCUITS

SERVINGS 15-18

PREP TIME 20 MINUTES + 30 MINUTES chilling time

COOK TIME 25-28 MINUTES

Ingredients

½ cup palm shortening

2 tablespoons honey

2 tablespoons full fat coconut milk

½ cup unsweetened applesauce

1 tablespoon minced fresh rosemary

½ cup coconut flour

½ cup tapioca flour

¼ teaspoon baking soda

½ teaspoon cream of tartar

¼ teaspoon salt

These biscuits are a perfect light addition to an afternoon cup of tea. A short, calming break with a warm drink and a little snack—what a treat!

1. Combine palm shortening, honey, coconut milk and applesauce in a food processor. Process on high 30 seconds. Set aside.

2. Using a large spoon, mix all remaining ingredients in a large bowl. Add applesauce mixture to dry ingredients and mix until soft dough forms. Using your hands, shape dough into a small log, approximately 9–10 inches in length. Wrap dough in plastic and refrigerate 30 minutes.

3. Preheat oven to 300 degrees. Remove dough from refrigerator and carefully slice into ½ inch disks. Place slices on a parchment-lined baking sheet and bake 25–28 minutes. Serve and enjoy!

NOTES

These little treats are very lightly sweetened and as such, are meant to be enjoyed more like a biscuit than a cookie.

CARROT CAKE MACAROONS

SERVINGS 15–18 MACAROONS

PREP TIME 10 MINUTES

COOK TIME 18–20 MINUTES

This particular recipe was a way to add a light and tasty dessert to Easter dinner.

Ingredients

2 cups unsweetened finely shredded coconut

1 teaspoon cinnamon

1 teaspoon ground ginger

¼ teaspoon mace

1 tablespoon coconut flour

⅛ teaspoon salt

⅛ teaspoon baking soda

2 large carrots, boiled until very soft

¼ cup coconut oil, melted

¼ cup honey

1 teaspoon pure vanilla extract

1. Preheat oven to 350 degrees. In a large bowl, combine dry ingredients. Set aside.

2. Puree carrots in a food processor. Add coconut oil, honey and vanilla. Process on high 30 seconds. Add wet ingredients to dry. Stir to combine.

3. Using a small, rounded cookie scoop, scoop dough and pack firmly, making bottom of macaroon flat. (If you do not have a cookie scoop you can pack two tablespoons of dough into your hand and form it into a small mound with a flat bottom.) Once formed, tap scoop so cookie falls into your hand. Place on a parchment-lined baking sheet. Repeat until all dough is used. Bake approximately 18–20 minutes. Allow to cool at least 5 minutes before transferring or macaroons will break apart. Serve and enjoy!

NOTES

These macaroons are based on recipes by Jenni Hulet of *The Urban Poser*.

RAISIN BREAD MACAROONS

SERVINGS 15–18 MACAROONS

PREP TIME 10 MINUTES

COOK TIME 18–20 MINUTES

Ingredients

2 cups unsweetened finely shredded coconut

1 teaspoon cinnamon

½ teaspoon ground ginger

1 tablespoon coconut flour

½ teaspoon salt

⅛ teaspoon baking soda

2 small, ripe bananas

¼ cup coconut oil, melted

¼ cup maple syrup

1 teaspoon pure vanilla extract

¼ cup raisins

This particular recipe happened after I walked through the bakery at a local grocery store and smelled fresh cinnamon-raisin bread. I immediately started longing for my pre-celiac days & got to work creating something I could safely enjoy.

1. Preheat oven to 350 degrees. In a large bowl, combine dry ingredients. Set aside.

2. Puree bananas in a food processor. Add coconut oil, maple syrup, vanilla and raisins. Process on high 30 seconds. Add wet ingredients to dry and stir to combine.

3. Using a small, rounded cookie scoop, scoop dough and pack firmly, making bottom of macaroon flat. (If you do not have a cookie scoop you can pack two tablespoons of dough into your hand and form it into a small mound with a flat bottom.) Once formed, tap scoop so cookie falls into your hand. Place on a parchment-lined baking sheet. Repeat until all dough is used. Bake approximately 18–20 minutes. Allow to cool at least 5 minutes before transferring or macaroons will break apart. Serve and enjoy!

NOTES

These macaroons are based on recipes by Jenni Hulet of *The Urban Poser*.

AVOCADO-LIME HAND PIES

SERVINGS 6

PREP TIME 30 MINUTES

COOK TIME 25-30 MINUTES

These are a little unusual, but I encourage you to go for it. They are a yummy treat, especially when you are still deep in the healing portion of your journey.

Filling Ingredients

1 ripe avocado

1½ tablespoons lime juice

¼ cup honey

Crust Ingredients

¾ cup tapioca flour

¾ cup coconut flour

¾ cup palm shortening

⅛ cup turbinado sugar (also called raw sugar)

1 ripe banana

¼ teaspoon salt

Filling

Put all ingredients in a food processor and process until smooth. Set aside.

Crust

1. Preheat oven to 350 degrees. Put all ingredients in a food processor and process until dough forms. Dust rolling pin with tapioca flour. Roll out dough on parchment paper to ⅛ inch thickness. Using a large round cookie cutter, cut out as many rounds as possible. Set aside. Reshape dough and cut again, repeating until all dough is used.

2. In center of 1 round, place 1 generous spoonful of filling. Place second round on top of first. Press around edges to close crust and then flute with a fork. Poke top of round with a fork. Repeat until all rounds are filled. Place on a parchment-lined baking sheet and bake 25–30 minutes. Serve and enjoy!

NOTES

Depending on humidity, dough may be too dry. If so, add 1 tablespoon full fat coconut milk (more if necessary, 1 tablespoon at a time). Dough should be soft and pliable.

ACCEPTANCE IN ILLNESS & HEALING

ILLNESS AND ACCEPTANCE

I have come a very long way since my third autoimmune diagnosis. I have been back and forth through all of the theorized stages of grief that can occur with a life-altering event (like chronic illness). I've also been through emotional stages that aren't as readily pinned down. I've experienced so much that is common on this path and other parts of it that have been very unique to me. Our journeys with autoimmune disease are both relatable and familiar, yet also extremely personal and private. One thing I am certain about is that reaching a level of acceptance seemed to be the key not just in regaining balance in my life, but in totally transforming it.

I cannot say that I am thankful for my autoimmune conditions. I mean honestly, can I truly be thankful that I can't have a cold beer on a hot day? Let's be real here. What I am grateful for is the journey. It has taught me so much, especially that I love me and the body I live in . . . diseases and all. I have come to view my AIs as battles worth fighting and getting up to meet those challenges each morning slowly changed me into something better than I would have otherwise been. Choosing to heal through diet and lifestyle lead me to an extraordinary recovery, but the moment I accepted chronic illness is really the moment I stopped being ill.

HEALING AND ACCEPTANCE

There were some bumps early in the process, but once healing took hold, acceptance on AIP was not at all hard for me. The reality was so clear I couldn't dismiss it. First, my mental and emotional health completely stabilized. The fog of depression lifted and I felt like myself again. Soon I was out-going and ready to laugh. The relief that my husband and daughter felt was evident the day my daughter ran to tell my husband I was smiling. Over the next three to six months, most of the worst physical symptoms diminished and then disappeared altogether. One year into the process I felt like I had been given a new body. My sense of appreciation for it was at least ten times greater than it had ever been.

Acceptance of my new AIP template also resulted in greater appreciation for my food. With all of my new found energy, I began putting a massive amount of effort into planning and preparing meals. If I could only eat a few things, I was determined to make it all delicious. I felt less and less limited by the restrictive diet and discovered that I enjoyed my food more and more. I found cooking with an eye on nutrient density and my ultimate health goals to be an awesome creative outlet. Eventually, I was able to re-introduce a few foods which opened up the possibilities for creativity even wider. That process continues for me and each successful reintroduction feels like a wonderful cause for celebration.

My time living in Africa reminded me of the simple things I took for granted in the U.S. I went through many of the stages of grief when I first moved there and recognized how much I had undervalued those things. Following AIP has been a very similar process. I am happy to report that I no longer undervalue what is on my plate. It is the most powerful medicine I have ever taken.

CHEATING

I don't like the word "cheat,"especially when applied to the movement toward better health. It gives the whole thing a bad vibe, but I don't have another word for "giving into temptation" so there we have it.

"Cheating," especially in the context of AIP, is human. Sticking to a nutrient dense diet is easy, but only if you live in an alternate reality where chips aren't basically designer drugs and all soda is flat, warm, and bitter. Choosing to adopt AIP is literally a revolutionary act. You are making a choice for your optimal health that is the antithesis to our culture right now. Yay, you! But the forces actively working against that choice are powerful. Powerful companies spend millions of dollars every day to carefully design and deceptively market food-like products that will undermine your health and line their pockets. Resistance is hard and to err is human.

Now, it sounds like I am saying this is way too hard so we shouldn't worry if we can't follow the protocol and have to cheat now and again. That's not what I'm saying. What I'm saying is, "I understand what we're up against is huge, but you're going to have to try – like really, really try." During the Elimination Phase, eating per the plan 99% of the time is not following the plan. It will not work. During reintroductions, suddenly veering off course can undermine what may be months or even years of focused work and makes identifying food sensitivities nearly impossible. So, again, I know it's hard. I truly and honestly and viscerally understand this so I'm going to help you by sharing some of the things I have learned through my own journey.

Ease in

All the members of my group programs and most of my individual clients know that I think taking your time to fully enter the Elimination Phase is smart. Remove one or two food groups at a time and work up to a full Elimination Phase. Cold turkey doesn't always work and self-motivation has to be extremely high. Small, gentle steps are much, much easier. "This week I'm giving up those donuts and next week I'll kick out the cheese." Ease in. You'll get there, no white-knuckles necessary.

Don't be weird

I'm telling you, do not be weird. If you act wishy-washy, uncomfortable, or uncertain about your food choices, then the people around you will also act weird. They won't take you seriously. They'll find it easy to dismiss your choices and soon you will find yourself minimizing the importance of your own health goals. Be confident when you inform others about the dietary plan you are following and emphasize how much you enjoy just being with them, even if you are not eating what they eat. "Aunt Gertrude, I am not eating lasagna these days, but I love being with you. I'm going to munch on some plantain chips while we chat."

Do the math

The elimination portion of AIP is not meant to last forever. Many people will find they are healed enough for reintroductions within months of beginning AIP and most will be ready within a year. That's 365 days. I was sick for a little over 11 years before I found this protocol. That's over 4,000 days of my life. I needed about a year in the Elimination Phase for my body to heal. Honestly, that is nothing compared to all the time that had already been spent in ever increasing pain and misery. Going 300 days without a slice of pizza is worth it to have 5,000 days of health.

Don't do FFFEF

Future Food Focused Event Fear. A lot of people use social events to justify "cheats." They are afraid to be seen as odd or to feel left out. The problem is that there is always another invite and there are almost no social gatherings without food. So what are your choices? A) Become a shut-in with 93 cats and a questionable internet boyfriend in Estonia. Or B) Don't give in to the fear. Don't constantly fret over another food-centered event. When an invite comes your way, make a plan and then go enjoy yourself. It can be done. I've done it at catered work conferences in other states, at catered weddings, at house parties, holiday dinners and on and on. Enjoy the lovely wedding and don't let not eating cake ruin it!

Frame it differently

You're not restricting your food, you are resetting your system with the help of a very specific food-based protocol. You are following nutritional and lifestyle-based ideals in order to restore your optimal health. Those with autoimmune conditions, like me, have more than the run-of-the-mill health challenges. When that is the case, it becomes even more important to adhere to certain ideals. "A candy bar is not the ideal I'm aiming for and it doesn't match what my body needs so I'm not going to eat it." It's all in how you frame it.

Stick to it

Take your time and listen to your body. Cook. Breathe. Heal. Think of this cookbook as another tool in helping you succeed. It includes delicious recipes that are strictly compliant with the Elimination Phase, but it also includes a sprinkling of recipes that are only allowed during various stages of the reintroduction process. If you aren't ready for reintroductions, don't let those recipes throw you off from your ultimate goal. Focus on the Elimination Phase recipes and know that good things are waiting for you. Keep healing in mind and look forward to the reintroduction process. When the time is right, you will know. I promise.

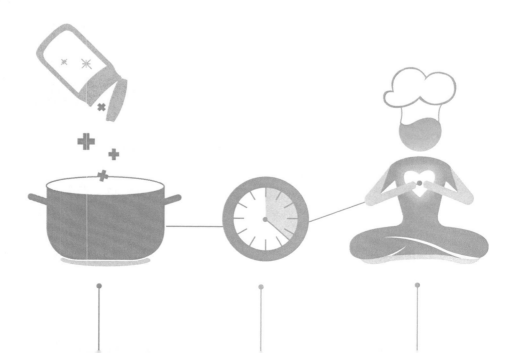

DREAMY ORANGE PUSH POPS

SERVINGS 15

PREP TIME 20 MINUTES + 1 HOUR chilling time

FREEZE TIME 20 MINUTES in ice cream maker **+ 4 HOURS** or overnight in freezer

! REQUIRED REINTRO
• VANILLA BEAN

Ingredients

2½ teaspoons unflavored gelatin

1 cup hot water, divided

2¼ cups unflavored coconut-milk yogurt

½ teaspoon orange zest

7 drops wild orange essential oil

2 tablespoons honey

2 whole vanilla beans, scraped

½ teaspoon pure vanilla extract

My sister is so creative! She loves essential oils and found a way to bring them into this cold, creamy treat. These pops are popular with kids, too! All my nieces and nephews loved them and our recipe tester said her kids (along with all the kids in her neighborhood) were begging for more.

1. Pour ¼ cup of water into a small bowl, sprinkle gelatin over to soften. Set aside.

2. Once softened, add gelatin, yogurt, remaining ¾ cup water, zest, essential oil, honey, vanilla bean seeds and vanilla extract to a food processor. Process on high until smooth. Transfer to a bowl or pitcher and allow to chill completely in refrigerator, approximately 1 hour.

3. Once chilled, pour mixture into the frozen core of automatic ice cream maker and follow manufacturer instructions for churning until almost done, approximately 20 minutes. Pour into silicone ice pop molds. Place in freezer until frozen solid, approximately 4 hours or overnight. Serve and enjoy!

NOTES

Coconut-milk yogurt can be found in health food stores and some grocery stores, but there are also many easy recipes online for making your own.

I prefer high-quality gelatin, like *Great Lakes* brand, and high-quality essential oils, like *doTerra*. Both can be found online.

Replacing the honey with maple syrup will make this a **FODMAP FREE** treat.

We asked our recipe testers, "Did you like this recipe?" One of them had the best reply ever. "Heck yes!" she said. "I love fall flavors and tend to make apple cider year-round, heat be damned. A sorbet is so perfect!" We couldn't agree more.

AUTUMN CIDER SORBET

SERVINGS 8

**PREP TIME 20 MINUTES +
1 HOUR chilling time**

**FREEZE TIME 20 MINUTES in
ice cream maker**

**! REQUIRED REINTRO
ALLSPICE AND NUTMEG**

Cider Ingredients

2 quarts apple juice (no sugar added)

4 cinnamon sticks

1½ tablespoons blackstrap molasses

2½ tablespoons honey

1 teaspoon whole cloves

1 teaspoon whole allspice

½ teaspoon ground ginger

¼ teaspoon ground nutmeg

Cranberry Sauce Ingredients

2 (10 ounce) bags cranberries, fresh
or frozen

½ cup water

½ cup + 1 tablespoon honey

Sorbet Ingredients

2 cups cider

2 cups cranberry sauce

Cider

1. Pour juice into a large pot. Add cinnamon sticks, molasses and honey. Bring to boil over medium-high heat. Add remaining spices. Return to boil and immediately reduce heat and simmer 10 minutes. Allow to cool.

2. Once cooled, strain cider into a large pitcher to remove clove, allspice and cinnamon sticks. Discard solids. Set cider aside.

Cranberry Sauce

1. Pour all ingredients into a medium pot and bring to boil. Reduce heat to medium and boil (slowly) 10 minutes. Cranberries will break down into pulp.

2. Cool and strain cranberries through a mesh sieve. Discard liquid.

Sorbet

1. Combine cider and cranberry sauce in a blender, blend until smooth. Transfer to a container and refrigerate until cold, approximately 1 hour.

2. Once cold, pour cranberry mixture into the frozen core of automatic ice cream maker and churn per manufacturer directions or until desired consistency. Serve and enjoy!

NOTES

Most ice creams require time in the freezer to "ripen" after churning. This extra freezer time is optional with this sorbet.

WHAT I DIDN'T KNOW

TEACHING WELLNESS TO THE NEXT GENERATION

If Only I Had Known

Honestly, if I had a dollar for every time I heard that from my clients or from myself, well, you know. "If only I had known this when I was younger . . ." "If only someone had told me..." "If only I had known I was sick..." As soon as my clients realize the power of diet and lifestyle on their disease, the "if onlys" set-in. And I get it. It's totally normal and understandable to think "if only" when a person undergoes the radical changes brought on by AIP. In my own journey, I always focused on how much damage to my body could have been avoided. At the very least, had I known of AIP earlier, the progression of my autoimmunity could have been slowed substantially and the risk of developing multiple AIs could have been mitigated. Although I have moved beyond mourning for my past, I think about these things often and can very much relate to my clients' grief.

Early Years and Forgiveness

It isn't like I had no training on healthy living. I spent my earliest years living on a homestead in rural Montana. My parents, grandparents, aunt and uncle raised animals and a huge variety of vegetables for food. My father hunted and fished. We even had raw milk from a local farmer. Butchering, harvesting, canning, dehydrating, fermenting, and exclusively homemade foods, which I was taught to prepare, were a very normal part of my childhood. Some of my fondest memories are of the cool, sandy floor of our huge underground root cellar, the shelves well-stocked with our homemade preserved foods.

   Somewhere along the way things began to change and by the time I was a teen, convenience foods had made their way into our lives. Then I went and used early adulthood to basically dismantle the awesome foundation of

My childhood home

real food built in my childhood. I know now, based on my own efforts, that it is a huge challenge to keep a traditional, healing foods approach going in our modern world. I'm sure my parents worked hard to maintain our diet despite a media blitz of health misinformation and without the benefit of knowing that the genes for celiac disease were inside me, just waiting to be turned on. And though, based on my earliest training, I could have probably made better decisions for myself, I didn't know what I didn't know. I forgive myself for every drive-thru, gas station, quick stop, and convenience store meal I ever ate . . . even the ones eaten at three a.m. that may or may not have included hot liquid "cheese" and beer chasers.

My Duty

Here's the thing though, I know now what I didn't know then. Maya Angelou said we should, ". . . do better, when we know better." I know how to restore and maintain health with food. I know that sleep matters profoundly. I know that sunshine and deep breaths and moving our bodies are absolutely necessary for every human being. I know so, so much more than I did, and that knowledge combined with all that stuff I learned as a little kid, leaves me with a big responsibility. One of the most important things I can do as a mother is teach my daughter wellness.

I cannot change the genetic code I gave her. I cannot change the way I previously fed our family. I cannot change that she's a teen now and sometimes not all that open to what mom has to say. What I can do, as her mother, is pass on as much of this powerful wellness knowledge as I possibly can. I can show her how to choose and prepare foods that keep her fit and fueled for life in a world that is rarely invested in her best health. Through my own actions I can reinforce for her that if she will lovingly care for it and provide it with the right tools, her body will heal itself. I can encourage her to question mainstream ideas about what is "healthy" and help her learn to advocate for true health. If I show her how this works, she may very well avoid the years of pain and confusion I endured.

My life was totally transformed by learning what I didn't know. My hope is that passing on that knowledge will ensure my daughter enjoys a strong, healthy life from the start. Is there any gift more valuable?

How Can I Actually Pass On This Knowledge?

So, everything I just wrote seems really great and all, but actually doing it is another story. I don't parent inside a magical snow globe where children eat heaping plates of grass-fed liver and kale prepared by enchanted elves for their breakfast (so I can sleep in, naturally) and then ride to school on unicorns with perfectly packed, adorable bento boxes filled with their Paleo lunches. I don't want to describe it because the reality of it is just too annoying, but basically, I parent in a situation exactly opposite the magical snow globe scenario I just painted. I'm willing to bet you are slogging through the same as I am. It's not all going to be perfect, certainly not when you have kids to guide through life, but that shouldn't stop us from trying. For that reason, here are my quick and dirty tips for dropping some wellness bombs on our (probably resistant) kids.

Start by feeding them breakfast. I know mornings are a hot mess for everyone, but the more I learn, the more convinced I am . . . good health starts with a big breakfast.

Plan lunches with them. Sit down together and have each child list his or her favorite meats, veggies, fruits, and treats (you can slowly work on Paleo-fying the treats). Let them pick one thing from each category and prepare very simple lunches from their choices.

Be prepared with afternoon snacks. Kids are ravenous beasts by the time three o'clock in the afternoon hits. Take a little time, once a week, to prepare a batch of something nutrient-dense to feed them. The name of the game is steady blood sugar levels.

Eat together. As often as possible and without distraction, take your meals together. Trim that schedule to make it happen. It is the main stage for showing them that real nutrition matters.

Consider compromise and teach them to cook. With kids 10 and older, some very carefully regulated compromise may be an appropriate way to acknowledge their developmental need for some decision-making independence and still win the majority of the nutritious food battles. Teaching them to cook will also feed the need for some independence and will help them develop confidence in their ability to care for themselves. Plus, it could be a big help to you!

Love your imperfect body. This applies to all kids, but especially to girls. Model that you appreciate your body and want to promote good health for yourself. Show that you value this above numbers on a scale, reflections in a mirror, or pleasing others.

Explain why. When your kids are old enough to understand, teach them the basics of nutrition. It might seem like they aren't paying attention, but those details will empower them to make healthy choices when they are off on their own contemplating instant ramen noodles versus organic, grass-fed beef stir-fry. We want them to make the best choice so we need to do our best to give them the tools to do so.

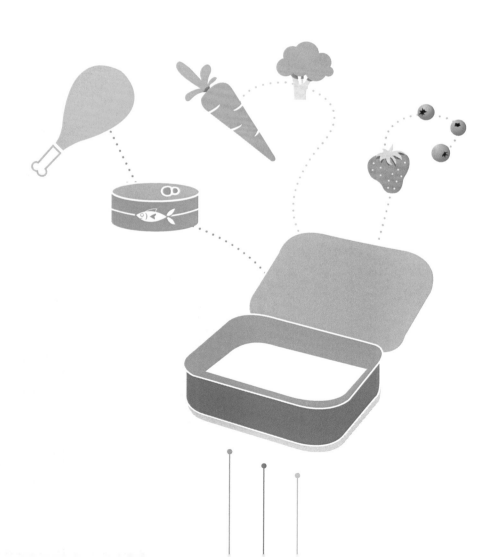

STAGE 2

BLUEBERRY CRUSH

SERVINGS 2

PREP TIME 5 MINUTES

! REQUIRED REINTRO
• HARD CIDER

Ingredients

2 lime wedges

¼ cup blueberries

2 tablespoons pomegranate juice

4 fresh mint leaves

1 (12 ounce) traditional dry hard apple cider

This drink is unique and refreshing, but remember to sip, not gulp. Even after successful reintroduction, too much alcohol is not a friend of AI disease.

In a tall glass, gently muddle limes and blueberries. Add pomegranate juice. Tear mint leaves in half, rub on rim of glass. Drop leaves into blueberry mixture. Half fill the glass with ice. Add hard cider to fill. Garnish with sprig of mint.

NOTES

Because they are often so much less sweet than mass-produced ciders, ciders from local ciderys are the best option for this drink. We like *Distillery Lane Ciderworks* in Jefferson, Maryland. For this recipe to meet the standards of a Stage 2 reintroduction, you'll need to limit your consumption to one eight-ounce glass. More would be considered a Stage 4 reintroduction. See Sarah Ballantyne's *The Paleo Approach* for guidance.

CHERRY-LIME SIPPERS

SERVINGS APPROX. 15 5 ounce glasses

PREP TIME 5 MINUTES + 2-3 HOURS chilling time

! REQUIRED REINTRO WINE

Ingredients

2 bottles (750 milliliters each) Riesling

1 bottle (750 milliliters) sparkling mineral water

1 (10 ounce) package frozen cherries

6 key limes, sliced

This drink looks so pretty served in a large glass pitcher on a late summer afternoon. Remember to sip, not gulp. Even after successful reintroduction, too much alcohol is not a friend of AI disease.

Combine Riesling and fruit in a large pitcher. Chill in refrigerator several hours or overnight. Immediately before serving, add sparkling mineral water, stir *gently*. Enjoy!

NOTES

For this recipe to meet the standards of a Stage 2 reintroduction, you'll need to limit your consumption to one five-ounce glass. More would be considered a Stage 4 reintroduction. See Sarah Ballantyne's *The Paleo Approach* for guidance.

STAGE 2

BANANA SPLIT MACAROONS

SERVINGS 15-18 MACAROONS

PREP TIME 10 MINUTES

COOK TIME 18-20 MINUTES

! REQUIRED REINTRO
CHOCOLATE

Ingredients

2 cups unsweetened finely shredded coconut

1 teaspoon cinnamon

½ teaspoon ground ginger

1 tablespoon coconut flour

½ teaspoon salt

⅛ teaspoon baking soda

2 small, ripe bananas

¼ cup coconut oil, melted

¼ cup maple syrup

1 teaspoon pure vanilla extract

2 dates, finely minced

6-9 cherries, pitted and sliced in half

¼ cup allergen-free chocolate chips

½ tablespoon coconut oil

This particular recipe happened after I decided I needed something banana-breadish and just kept going all the way to banana-splitish!

1. Preheat oven to 350 degrees. In a large bowl, combine dry ingredients. Set aside.

2. Puree bananas in a food processor. Add remaining wet ingredients plus dates to food processor. Process on high 30 seconds. Add wet ingredients to dry. Stir to combine.

3. Using a small, rounded cookie scoop, scoop dough and pack firmly, making bottom of macaroon flat. (If you do not have a cookie scoop you can pack two tablespoons of dough into your hand and form it into a small mound with a flat bottom.) Once formed, tap scoop so cookie falls into your hand. Place on a parchment-lined baking sheet. Using back of cookie scoop, very gently press down on top of macaroon to make a small "thumb" print. Repeat until all dough is used. Bake approximately 18–20 minutes. Allow to cool at least 5 minutes before transferring or macaroons will break apart.

4. While macaroons are baking, add chocolate chips and coconut oil to a small saucepan. Melt over very low heat, stirring to incorporate coconut oil.

5. Once macaroons have cooled, place 1 cherry half in each "thumb" print and drizzle with chocolate. Allow chocolate to cool and harden before serving. Enjoy!

NOTES

For allergen-free chocolate chips, I prefer *Enjoy Life* brand, which can be purchased at most health food and mainstream grocery stores.

These macaroons are based on recipes by Jenni Hulet of The *Urban Poser*.

STAGE 2

LEMON BAR ICE CREAM

SERVINGS 6-8

PREP TIME 1 HOUR + 2 HOURS chilling time

FREEZE TIME 20 MINUTES in ice cream maker

! REQUIRED REINTRO
  BUTTER

Cookie Crust Ingredients

½ cup palm shortening

3 tablespoons honey

½ cup coconut flour

½ cup + 1 tablespoon tapioca flour

2 tablespoons full fat coconut milk

¼ cup unsweetened applesauce

¼ teaspoon baking soda

½ teaspoon cream of tartar

¼ teaspoon salt

Lemon Filling Ingredients

5 tablespoons butter

½ cup full fat coconut milk

2 tablespoons arrowroot flour

3 tablespoons honey

1 teaspoon lemon zest

6 tablespoons lemon juice

pinch of salt

Ice Cream Ingredients

2 (15 ounce) cans full fat coconut milk

2 teaspoons lemon zest

¼ cup honey

This is probably my favorite recipe creation. It is a bit of a labor of love, but so delicious!

Cookie Crust

Preheat oven to 300 degrees. Combine all ingredients in a large bowl. Spread dough thinly over a large, parchment-lined baking sheet. Bake 25–30 minutes or until browned. Cool. Crumble cooled crust into bite size pieces by hand. Set-aside.

Lemon Filling

Melt butter in a medium pot over low heat. In a small dish, mix arrowroot flour and coconut milk. Stir into melted butter. Add honey, lemon zest, lemon juice and salt to butter mixture, stirring constantly until a low boil is reached. Cook 3 minutes, stirring constantly. Transfer to a clean bowl and allow to cool completely in refrigerator.

Ice Cream

1. Pour all ingredients into a medium saucepan and simmer over low heat. Stir until honey dissolves. Transfer to a bowl or pitcher and allow to cool completely in refrigerator.

2. Once cooled, pour into the frozen core of automatic ice cream maker and follow manufacturer directions for churning. During final 3–5 minutes of churning, add cookie crumbles and lemon filling to ice cream. Enjoy immediately as soft-serve (which is the way I like it!) or transfer to a freezer-safe container and freeze at least 2 hours for optimal ripening.

WHO'S YOUR FARMER?

Celiac disease woke me up to how food is the tie that binds. It connects us in a primal and unavoidable way. My food awakening led me to the understanding that eating a healing diet meant sourcing food that was as whole and unprocessed as possible. For me, "as whole and unprocessed as possible" also meant local. Lucky me, finding local farms producing meats and produce also lead to special new friendships. An incredible side of food was opened up for me and with it came an enormous appreciation for farmers.

Week after week, I slowly got to know the farmers producing the food I was buying and soon those relationships became invaluable. I now know the women growing the food my family eats. I know how hard they work. I know their families, their stories. I know what put them on the path to the farming life. I know their practices and approaches to raising animals and produce. I know their plans for the future of their farms. I rely on these farmers for food and they rely on me for income. That shared responsibility, combined with true friendship, has made me deeply invested in my farmers and the land in my community. Wendell Berry wrote that, "Eating is an agricultural act." I could not agree more. The more I am able, from a practical and financial standpoint, to invest in my local farms, the better I feel. More and more, my plate accurately reflects my values.

To all small, family farmers, most especially "my" farmers, Nora Crist and Kelly Hensing, thank you for taking on one of the most important jobs on our planet. Thank you for producing delicious, high-quality food that feeds us, body and mind. Thank you for getting up with the sun and working until well after dark. Thank you for treating your livestock with respect and love and for knowing the true value of healthy soil and clean water. We are lucky that our "agricultural act" can begin with you.

So, who's your farmer?

Photo by Lise Metzger

RESOURCES

When I began my journey, I learned from and collaborated with the five women behind the websites listed below. Together we represented the entire AIP blogging community and soon our little group formed a solid support system for each other. Since that time, the community has grown by leaps and bounds. I am happy to say that if you do a little googling, you will now find well over 30 sites (and growing) dedicated to healing autoimmune disease using the Autoimmune Protocol. You are not alone on your walk to wellness.

The Paleo Mom

Autoimmune Paleo

Phoenix Helix

A Clean Plate

Nutrisclerosis

BOOK SHELF ESSENTIALS

Print (available on Amazon)

The Autoimmune Paleo Cookbook

The Paleo Approach: Reverse Autoimmune Disease and Heal Your Body

The Paleo Approach Cookbook: A Detailed Guide to Heal Your Body and
   Nourish Your Soul

Ebooks

The FODMAP Free Paleo Breakthrough

28 Days of AIP

Reintroducing Foods on the Paleo Autoimmune Protocol

175

MAKE IT YOURSELF

Homemade Coconut Milk Yogurt
Bone Broth

If you are using this book in print format, a simple Google search of the above terms will lead you to recipes for making these foods at home.

WHERE TO FIND IT

Fatworks (duck fat, tallow, lard)
Red Boat Fish Sauce (gluten-free fish sauce)
Coconut Aminos (soy sauce substitute)
Bob's Red Mill (arrowroot flour & tapioca flour)
Edward & Sons Trading Co. (Let's Do Organic coconut flour)
Northwest Wild Foods (huckleberries)
Jackson Hole Buffalo Meat Co. (free-range elk)
U.S. Wellness Meats (grass-fed/pastured meats & wild-caught seafood)
Tropical Traditions (coconut oil & palm shortening)
Great Lakes Gelatin (grass-fed gelatin & collagen)
doTerra (essential oils)
Enjoy Life (allergen-free chocolate chips)
Salt Fire and Time (bone broth)

If you are using this book in print format, a simple Google search of the above terms will lead you to quality online retailers.

AUTHOR'S NOTE

I am indebted to Sarah Ballantyne for her extensive work on the Autoimmune Protocol, the American Autoimmune Related Diseases Association for working to increase public awareness of autoimmune diseases, and Australia's Monash University for their detailed research on FODMAPs. It is their work that I have referenced in writing this book.

GRATITUDE

I have many to thank in writing this cookbook, so many that a list seems the best way to let the gratitude flow.

1—I want to thank God. I have doubted Your will for my life many, many times, but always, without fail, the most amazing things have come from my darkest moments.

2—I want to thank my husband, David Alt, and my daughter, Maggee Hunt. You are the reason . . . for all of it. You have supported me through a year-long process, boosted my confidence when I was afraid to put this out there, and eaten a lot of food in the name of "testing." Thank you for letting me follow this dream. I love you both.

3—I want to thank my parents. My mother, Lori Miller, for always encouraging me in my endeavors, expressing your love for me and for creating the beautiful aprons featured in this book. My father, Gary Clark, for instilling in me an unflagging work ethic. And my stepmother, Lynnette Clark, for your excited support of this project and your expert help in the kitchen.

4—I want to thank my sister, Jenifer Beehler. I knew you were the right partner for this project and the countless "brain dump" sessions confirmed it. You have been creative, productive, and fun, but most of all, you did not laugh when I said I wanted to do it.

5—I want to thank my photographer, Toni Snelling. You believed in the ideals behind this food and willingly learned a whole new set of photography skills for the project. None of this would have happened without your vision and professional contribution.

6—I want to thank my friend and colleague, Mickey Trescott. Your inspiration and support from conception to completion has been absolutely invaluable to this project. I am grateful for and admire your contribution to this community and your very rare and genuine spirit. I count myself lucky to be "in the battle" with you. I also want to thank my friend, Sarah Ballantyne. The ripple effect of your research and writing on the Autoimmune Protocol is incalculable. I am honored to work with The Paleo Mom Consulting and grateful to you for the way your work has completely transformed my life and informed this project.

7—I want to thank my editor, Anne Hedgecock. I am a writer who can't be bothered with grammar or the art of the single space! Thank goodness for your careful eye and guidance on everything from recipe formatting to word choice. You have given my work professional polish. I also want to thank my designer, Chelsey Luther. Your creative spark and uniquely inspired vision turned my dream into reality. What more can I say? Thank you.

8—I want to thank my farmers, Nora Crist of Clark's Farm in Ellicott City, Maryland and Kelly Hensing of Hensing's Hilltop Acres in Dayton, Maryland, who graciously donated all of the meat featured in this book. I cannot emphasize enough how much I respect your work. No farms, no food.

9—I want to thank my father-in-law, David Alt Sr., for your legal advice and guidance, and my mother-in-law, Veronica Alt, for your unwavering enthusiasm for this project.

10—I want to thank Troy Evans for donating the gorgeous wood backgrounds used in the food photography, Ted Kim for providing a beautiful studio space for the portrait photography, and my grandmother, Katie Alt, for the incredible setting of the family home for additional portrait photography.

11—I want to thank the Institute for Integrative Nutrition for providing an accessible, solid foundation from which to launch my career. I hope my work plays a crucial role in the school's overall mission of improving the health and happiness of those around us and through that, transforming the world.

12—I want to thank an army of friends and family members for their support, in everything from donating your dishes, your dishwashing skills, your handmade potholders, your unique taste buds and honest opinions, your recipe testing, your editing skills, your unending (and early) encouragement, and even your last elk tenderloin (a precious thing for a Montanan family).

13—And last, but certainly not least, I want to thank you. If you are reading this cookbook, chances are you or someone you love is fighting chronic illness. Your willingness to try a brand new diet and lifestyle in order to heal has energized each step of this project. I wish you wellness.

Sincerely—

Angie Alt

ABOUT

THE AUTHORS

Angie Alt lives outside Washington, D.C. (but her heart belongs to Montana) with her incredibly supportive husband and teenage daughter. As a certified health coach she guides individual and group clients on the autoimmune journey with powerful diet & lifestyle techniques. She has been blogging regularly since 2009, with a special focus on mixing "data with soul." In her spare time, she enjoys nature walks, reminiscing about her days as a world traveler, and obsessively visiting "tiny home" websites. As an autoimmune warrior herself, Angie hopes this project will connect people to their autoimmune answers and help them achieve wellness with balance. You can find her on Facebook and Instagram.

Jenifer Beehler lives in Billings, Montana with her husband and wildcat six-year-old son. Jenifer began her career as a stylist in 2002 and has loved helping each one of her clients experience her own inner beauty. She has fun experimenting in the kitchen with flavor and texture combinations that will appeal to her "standard American" family, snowboarding (or falling) in the mountain ranges of Montana, and spending time laughing with friends. Her intention in collaborating on this project is to help create approachable, real food that anyone can make without the "diet food" feel.

THE PHOTOGRAPHER

Photo by Ronnie Ruiz

Toni Snelling lives in Billings, Montana. She holds a bachelor's degree in photography with an emphasis in photojournalism. She is also a wildland firefighter, an EMT with an area hospital, and an EMT on an ambulance crew. When Toni is not taking photos, she can be found practicing Crossfit, backpacking with family in the Montana wilderness, and canning huge amounts of jam and apple butter with her grandma. Her goal in taking on this project was to show others the beauty of real, healing food. Toni can be found on Facebook and on her blog at **www.toniraephotographyblog.com**.